T0329338

"Since the onset of COVID-19, the issues of anxiety and related social and emotional challenges have become even more pronounced. However, it is not productive to simply fret and wait for professionals to intervene while claiming it is not our responsibility. This much-needed book brings together an expert in professional learning, a psychologist, and a principal who has firsthand experience with these issues. They speak candidly and offer guidance on how to address the social and emotional aspects of learning.

The book delves into the subject matter with great depth and richness. It explores concepts such as projection, containment, and attachment to provide explanations. It also sheds light on understanding extreme behaviors, managing panic, anger, self-harm, depression, and school refusal. Moreover, it tackles critical issues such as anxiety and depression.

Equally important, the book presents a highly positive narrative about the creation of a nurturing and compassionate school environment. It emphasizes the significance of trust and communication, the promotion of teacher clarity, the reduction of cognitive load, student-focused feedback, and the cultivation of self-efficacy, containment, and overall well-being.

Unlike many who despair over this situation and advocate for an influx of medical professionals in schools, Clarke, Evans, and Moss argue for an increased focus on successful learning. They propose the concept of a 'team around the child' within a harmonious culture characterized by calmness, care, and compassion. They believe that teaching can be an immensely rewarding and joyful experience, and that students in our schools can be liberated from anxiety. By doing so, they will not only be prepared to learn but also able to experience the delight of confident self-efficacy.

This is the resource I have been waiting for – how to help educators integrate social and emotional learning as core to the role of schools."

John Hattie, *Melbourne Laureate Professor Emeritus*

"Stress is what happens when the demands on you which you accept or cannot avoid exceed the resources you think you have to cope. Education is fundamentally about building young people's capacity and appetite for coping with demands, especially challenge, change and uncertainty – and thereby *reducing* stress! Schools that *increase* net stress rather than reducing it are therefore not doing their job (however good their exam results). Stress and anxiety are systemic problems, not puddles of individual unhappiness that need mopping up by caring teachers and counsellors. This marvelous new book takes this pressing issue by the horns and shows how whole school cultures can and must change to meet the challenges of complex and turbulent times."

Professor Guy Claxton, *author of the* Future of Teaching: and the Myths that Hold It Back

"I found this book fascinating, especially for the way it blends teaching and learning with therapeutic perspectives. The insights of an experienced headteacher, a therapist and a well-known education expert are woven seamlessly together, to convey admirably how we can make school a place of psychological safety for all – for adults as well as children. There are vivid examples of brilliant classroom practice and many engaging 'stories' about real children. The book will be welcomed by everyone who is concerned about the rising tide of mental health needs in our children, and the increasing stress experienced by teachers and leaders."

Jean Gross CBE, *Independent consultant, Early Intervention Foundation Associate, Director of The SEAL Community (www.sealcommunity.org), Associate Fellow at University of Warwick*

"This is one of those books which every teacher needs to read especially as mental health concerns are growing in our classrooms. I found it incredibly useful, relatable and I thoroughly enjoyed dipping in and out and reflecting against my practice and the characters that I teach. I cannot see things improving quickly with regards to young people's anxiety, but maybe now through this book, we will have some ideas to help our students gain the support they need."

Andria Zafirakou

Understanding and Reducing Anxiety in the Primary School

Everyone working in education, and beyond, is fully aware of the current mental health crisis for pupils. *Understanding and Reducing Anxiety in the Primary School* combines the expert knowledge of a specialist in formative assessment, a child and adolescent psychotherapist and an outstanding headteacher to address how we may tackle this issue and improve the well-being of children in our schools. Formative assessment, one of the key techniques explored within this book, has explicit links with reducing anxiety: raising children's belief in their ability to achieve and giving them clear frameworks of learning intentions and success criteria as well as in-the-moment feedback so that they are reassured and able to voice any worries while they are working.

Writing in a practical and accessible manner, the authors unpack the psychology behind issues related to students' mental health and provide illustrative, relatable anecdotes and helpful strategies to support a positive, anxiety-free learning environment.

The book is divided into four distinct sections:

◆ Why is everyone so anxious and what can we do about it?
◆ Understanding and dealing with extreme behaviour
◆ Supporting the learning to reduce anxiety
◆ Creating a containing and compassionate school

This is a must read for anyone working in a primary school. Readers will benefit from learning strategies to reduce the anxiety of the children they work with and to support the wellbeing of the wider educational community.

Shirley Clarke holds a wealth of experience in educational research, including 10 years at the Institute of Education, UCL, and from 23 years of action research teams across the world. She is a multi-bestselling author, including *Outstanding Formative Assessment* and *Visible Learning Feedback* co-authored with John Hattie.

Angela Evans is a Child and Adolescent Psychoanalytic Psychotherapist with extensive experience of working with children, young people and families, individually and with the wider system around them. She worked for 20 years for the National Health Service (NHS) Child and Adolescent Mental Health Service (CAMHS), specialising in Looked After Children.

Kate Moss, with a therapy background, is an experienced headteacher and supervisor for education professionals. She also acts as Facilitator for the National Professional Qualifications for Leadership (Behaviour and Culture) (NPQLBC) and Church of England Foundation For Educational Leadership (CEFEL) in addition to Expert Coaching for National Professional Qualification for Senior Leadership (NPQSL) CEFEL.

Understanding and Reducing Anxiety in the Primary School

Theory and Practice for Building a Compassionate Culture for All Educators and Children

Shirley Clarke, Angela Evans and Kate Moss

Routledge
Taylor & Francis Group

LONDON AND NEW YORK

Designed cover image: Front cover illustration by Dani Pasteau

First published 2024
by Routledge
4 Park Square, Milton Park, Abingdon, Oxon OX14 4RN

and by Routledge
605 Third Avenue, New York, NY 10158

Routledge is an imprint of the Taylor & Francis Group, an informa business

British Library Cataloguing-in-Publication Data
A catalogue record for this book is available from the British Library

Library of Congress Cataloging-in-Publication Data
Names: Clarke, Shirley, author. | Evans, Angela, 1956- author. |
Moss, Kate, 1967- author.
Title: Understanding and reducing anxiety in the primary school : theory and practice for building a compassionate culture for all educators and children / Shirley Clarke, Angela Evans and Kate Moss.
Description: Abingdon, Oxon ; New York, NY : Routledge, 2024. |
Includes bibliographical references and index.
Identifiers: LCCN 2023057643 (print) | LCCN 2023057644 (ebook) |
ISBN 9781032593791 (hardback) | ISBN 9781032593784 (paperback) |
ISBN 9781003454434 (ebook)
Subjects: LCSH: School children--Psychology. | School children--Mental health. |
Anxiety in children. | School environment--Psychological aspects.
Classification: LCC LB3430 .C56 2024 (print) | LCC LB3430 (ebook) |
DDC 155.42/4--dc23/eng/20240207
LC record available at https://lccn.loc.gov/2023057643
LC ebook record available at https://lccn.loc.gov/2023057644

ISBN: 978-1-032-59379-1 (hbk)
ISBN: 978-1-032-59378-4 (pbk)
ISBN: 978-1-003-45443-4 (ebk)

DOI: 10.4324/9781003454434

Typeset in Palatino
by KnowledgeWorks Global Ltd.

Contents

Foreword

This is a powerful book – a must read for primary and early-years colleagues everywhere. Reading this made me think back over my time in schools. Throughout my career as a teacher, I have sought to create the containing classroom culture that is described here so powerfully by Shirley, Angela and Kate. Many of my actions were instinctive, but increasingly my vision, values and purpose were shaped by study, research and academic coaching.

I came into education because I wanted to make things better. Initially my main aim was that the children who I taught would know they were valued and listened to. I wanted my classroom to be a safe space for all. Of course, I wanted the children to learn, but my priority was that we would support each other as a collective. I was not always successful in this endeavour, but I kept trying to find a way through for every child. 'Swimming against the tide' has always been part of my restless ambition to improve education. From the earliest days, I resisted labelling and ranking children, seeing the impact that such action would have upon motivation and self-belief. When I moved from teaching to leading a school, the pressures for performativity were even higher, but so was my own imperative to create a 'listening school'. I was driven by the need to create a school where learning would be irresistible, both for children and teachers. To do this, I knew the wider experience of attending school, working there or being part of the local community should be a positive, affirming one.

It is easy to say that the school vision was to provide inclusive education, but this was a true aim. During my time as a teacher and school leader, I was involved in research that led to publication of the 'Learning without Limits' (Hart, Dixon, Drummond and McIntyre, 2004; Peacock, 2016; Swann, Peacock, Hart and Drummond, 2012). This work challenged notions of 'fixed ability'. It challenged the dominant practice of ability grouping within primary classrooms that led inexorably to setting in the secondary phase. It challenged the value of reward systems that lead to temporary extrinsic motivation. So as a school leader, backed and inspired by this research, I set about building a community where children were trusted and were constantly given opportunities to surprise us.

This book focuses on relationships between children and their schools; the impact of extreme behaviours on staff, those charged with responding and managing outbursts, is explored, valued and understood. In my experience, another one of the most stressful parts of being a teacher and leader is containing the emotions of parents and families. Confrontations with angry parents were rare but stand out in my memory as times when I acknowledged high levels of anxiety. One particular example comes to mind:

> *During the first few weeks of my headship I had a meeting with a mother who was angry with me because her seven year old daughter had not had her reading book changed by her teacher for several days. The school was under pressure at the time as an HMI (Her Majesty's Inspectorate) visit was imminent. Instead of waiting for Mrs F to say everything that she wanted to about her complaint I interrupted her and tried to explain the situation from my point of view. Instead of helping, this escalated the onslaught and resulted in the parent storming out of my office declaring that she was going to report me to Ofsted.*
>
> *That weekend, having reflected on this incident, I went shopping with my daughter to buy items for my new office. I came across an ornamental wooden crocodile. It was an attractive, smiley crocodile which I thought would look nice on my coffee table. Importantly, it was smiling with its mouth tight shut. I realised that this would provide an excellent reminder to me next time I had an angry person on my room that I should empathise, listen carefully and where possible stay quiet.*

I have shared that anecdote many times to conference audiences, but it is only after reading this book that I realise that the crocodile, bought on a fun shopping trip with my daughter, also represented my family's support for the work I was doing as a headteacher. I was contained by their love and commitment to my work.

In creating a 'learning without limits' school, I quickly realised that I needed to build a team who could work alongside me to contain the needs of our community. I can see now that this was an act of self-protection; there is no point having a bold inclusive vision if the work is personally difficult and ultimately damaging. As a team, we worked together to build professional knowledge about therapeutic support, and we embraced a multi-agency approach, employed an art therapist, a staff counsellor and family support workers. Our culture of openness meant that we embraced a curriculum that centred around nature, the outdoors, the wider world. Many of these strategies are discussed later.

Particular children stand out in my memory as those for whom school was not always comfortable – children such as those described within this book who demanded to be noticed, to be treated differently and ultimately to be loved. I can still visualise and name these children. – characters who I spent hours worrying about, reacting to and planning for. Ultimately, however, when I look back over decades of teaching, it is my relationship with these children that I cherish the most.

My decision to leave headship to take forward leadership of the Chartered College of Teaching was driven by what I saw as a collective need for greater self-efficacy across our profession. In particular, when I attended the inaugural #LearningFirst conference at Sheffield Hallam, I realised the transformative potential of collaboration and of sharing practice in a safe non-judgmental space. The kind of atmosphere I valued within my classroom as a teacher and across my school as a headteacher was replicated on that day by hundreds of colleagues from across the country who came together to share their approach to assessment that put children first. Shirley Clarke was present and indeed led a vote of thanks for the beginning of what has become a movement to enhance professionalism.

I am passionate about the importance of *phronesis* – enhancing wisdom with intellectual professional knowledge. This book serves that purpose exactly. We are helped to reflect on what may cause school anxiety both individually and collectively. Seeking to draw upon psychoanalysis and psychotherapy combined with the wisdom of education leadership and research, we are offered trusted, informed advice. Greater professional awareness of the manner in which anxiety can become heightened, and understanding of how to best manage this, will hopefully help more schools to build a compassionate culture where everyone (children and adults) knows they are safe and valued.

Teachers transform lives – but never let it be said that this is an easy thing to do. There is so much within this book to celebrate, practical wisdom combined with vision and heart. I know you will enjoy reading this, and I hope you find much within your own practice that resonates strongly.

Alison Peacock

References

Hart, S., Dixon, A., Drummond, M.J. and McIntyre, D. (2004) *Learning without Limits*. London: Open University Press.

Peacock, A.M. (2016) *Creating Learning without Limits*. London: Open University Press.

Swann, M., Peacock, A., Hart, S. and Drummond, M.J. (2012) *Creating Learning without Limits*. London: Open University Press.

Acknowledgements

Shirley Clarke

I have been totally inspired by working with Dr Angela Evans and Kate Moss. This book has been an absolute meeting of minds. I am fortunate to have known Angela for many years and seen the impact of her work with troubled children and, while videoing a teacher at Clearwater School in Gloucester, discovered that the almost tangible, contained and compassionate culture was the impact of Kate's deliberate and strategic vision. Thank you both for joining with me in creating this book which we so passionately hope will help teachers and children to overcome at least some of the anxieties we see ever growing in our schools. Our collective love of education, children, learning and writing has been the thread running through the book, and it has been a joy and an easy process for us to write together.

As always, I am indebted to the thousands of teachers across the world I have been lucky enough to work with, linking theory with practical strategies. The teaching and learning frameworks in Part III of this book, which powerfully reduce anxiety in the classroom, draw on those teachers' experiences. This book is dedicated to you all for your continued love of the best profession in the world and your endless quest to be the best you can be. I want to take this opportunity, also, to thank my beloved niece, Ellie, for qualifying this year as a primary teacher. I am so proud of you, and I know you will positively impact so many young lives through your career.

Thank you to Langford Primary School, Hammersmith and Fulham, for the inspirational art curriculum graphic and to The Reach Academy, Feltham, for the most accessible knowledge organiser I've ever seen.

Thanks go to John Hattie for endless inspiration and a helpful critical review, Alison Peacock for her foreword, Katherine Muncaster for also giving sound advice and finally Sarah Le Templier, who not only reviewed the book for us but is a key contributor to two of the chapters. Sarah was a member of one of my learning teams and one of the teachers I wanted to video in her classroom. She is an exceptional teacher with an exemplary classroom culture of caring compassion coupled with rigorous teaching.

Thank you Sarah for all the curriculum links you provided for opening up discussion with children about difficult emotions in Chapter 13 as well as your written descriptions in Chapter 15 of your use of texts linking literacy learning intentions with class discussion about emotions. These will be so helpful for teachers to see exactly how to capitalise on rich, emotive texts.

Thanks also to Bruce Roberts, our Routledge editor, who I worked with on 'Visible Learning Feedback' co-authored with John Hattie. After the ease of working with you before, I knew you would be the perfect person for such an important book. It has to be accessible in every way, to reach as many teachers as possible, and you have absolutely made that happen.

I finally want to thank my husband John and our daughter, Katy, now 19, for your love and support.

Angela Evans

My immense thanks go to Shirley Clarke for approaching me with her concern about rising mental health in schools. Shirley's continual openness to finding new ways to help educate and empower children was apparent as we spoke together about the subject. Through Shirley, I met Kate Moss, whose inspiring leadership and vision for her school encompass her love for education and good mental health. This was truly a meeting of minds. We had all trodden different but interweaving paths in education and in enabling children to feel good about themselves so that they can all reach their best potential. Our joint passion for children's wellbeing and development led to this book. I have loved writing with these two women, who have both inspired me and from whom I have learnt so much. Special thanks to Shirley for so skilfully editing this book and generously sharing her writing experience.

I would like to thank my teachers, mentors, analysts and supervisors along the way, from my early training in teaching, my further training in therapeutic teaching approaches and my training in Child and Adolescent Psychotherapy. The many people who have helped me and continue to help me have been invaluable. They have given me encouragement when I wavered, built my confidence, facilitated my growth and helped me to be the best I can be. Special thanks to Dr Leslie Ironside, my steady unwavering guide for the last 20 years.

Thanks to Gill David for introducing me to the world of art therapists, which has continued to inform and nurture me as I have taught and examined many art therapy students over the years. As much as the students have learnt from me, so I have learnt from them about the immense value of the Arts on mental health. My supervisees from many different fields of therapy are also a constant source of learning for me. I thank you all.

I have been lucky enough to work with some wonderfully resourceful, diligent and resilient colleagues as I have traversed the path to helping severely traumatised young people. I have learnt how vital it is to have a strong team around a child who has not had early love and containment. In increasingly difficult, under-resourced services, my colleagues from clinical settings, education, social services and residential homes have retained their love for and commitment to the children and young people with whom they work. Thank you for your dedication and compassion.

In teaching, caring for and giving therapy to countless children and their families, I have learnt from every one of them. How to teach a class of children whilst letting them know you're on their side. How to reach out to the children who need the adults the most. And how to enter children's inner worlds with respect, to hold their hands as we encounter painful and frightening memories and to know when to speak, when to listen, when to confront, when to let my tears fall and when to let the children go. It has been a truly humbling experience. I am very grateful and honoured to have known them.

Finally, my thanks go to my husband Andy for his unfailing help, patience and support. To my loyal friends who have had endless conversations with me about my work and have shared their wisdom and supported me throughout. And to my ever-growing family, my greatest teachers, for your love.

Kate Moss

I have been privileged to work with, and learn from, so many inspiring and talented people within the education world – people in many roles who are committed, hardworking and always have children's best interests at the forefront of their minds. Without knowing it, you have all been a part of this book as I reflected and grew as a teacher. This could not be more true of my amazing team at Clearwater Primary Academy who were willing to bravely follow me into the unknown world of a brand new school and make it come alive with warmth, humour and vibrancy. You are an inspiration daily. To everyone creating, contributing and investing in the education of our young people, thank you.

I am also indebted to two people who have been such a positive, knowledgeable and supportive influence over the years, Jo Grills and John Coles; your wisdom and laughter are massively appreciated. Thank you.

I was delighted to find myself working with Shirley Clarke and Dr Angela Evans, women at the peak of their careers who have pursued excellence in their respective fields. Through many conversations, it was clear we all held a common goal, that of creating compassionate learning environments for pupils and staff alike. Thank you both for your in-depth knowledge, your enthusiasm and belief. Your kindness, guidance and friendship throughout have been an added and valued bonus.

I have been lucky to have worked not just in education but in the world of psychological and mental health. The knowledge I gained in these fields is immensely valuable in my current work. One of the key people who developed my understanding is Professor Steve Peters. Thank you Steve, my time working for you at Chimp Management was transformational and had a direct impact when creating my own compassionate culture.

Finally, I must thank everyone in my gorgeous family but especially my husband Adrian and my sons, Joe and Harry for your encouragement, giggles and being my world.

Introduction

Our aims for this book

Everyone in education, and beyond, is fully aware of the rise in mental health issues in our schools, exacerbated by the Covid pandemic and its post-traumatic stress disorder (PTSD) effect. There are now courses for educators and a wealth of literature to try to make sense of it all, so how is this book going to be different? Combining the expertise of an academic, a psychotherapist and a school leader, we explore the psychology behind the issues and outline a wealth of practical strategies for an integrated, classroom and school-based approach, creating an anxiety-free learning environment.

As the title suggests, this book is intended to support the development of a caring, educational environment so that the day-to-day business of teaching is at the fore. We, the authors, would like to remind you that any behaviour, disclosures or conversations that lead you to have safeguarding concerns in your place of work **must** be reported to your designated safeguarding lead or equivalent, and your own safeguarding policy must be followed. If any issues brought by children affect you, speak to colleagues or to a senior manager. You don't need to feel alone with it.

Who we are

Shirley Clarke

I am known for the practical application of the principles of formative assessment, still the most significant thing we can do in schools to raise attainment and develop confident learners. I was a teacher, a primary mathematics advisor, a test writer and a lecturer and have been working with teachers for many years, across the world, to develop formative assessment

DOI: 10.4324/9781003454434-1

understanding and its strategies, via training, action research groups and my publications.

Dr Angela Evans

I am fortunate to have known Angela for many years. Her expertise is child and adolescent mental health and she worked for National Health Service (NHS) Child and Adolescent Mental Health Services (CAMHs) for 20 years, as well as having a background in care settings and teaching as a Special Educational Needs and Disabilities Coordinator (SENDCo). In discussion about my work, we realized that there are many explicit helpful links with psychoanalytic and psychological theory, and awareness of these can significantly reduce anxiety in the classroom. I had been thinking of elements such as learning intentions and success criteria and on-the-move feedback purely as learning and teaching frameworks but, with Angela's insights, could see the possibilities for helping our children thrive more effectively. She writes with expert knowledge and insight, illustrated by powerful anecdotes of her own experiences working with teachers and troubled children.

Kate Moss

In the summer of 2022, I was lucky enough to visit Clearwater Academy Primary School in Gloucester, to video an exceptional teacher, and was struck by the apparent lack of any mental health issues in the school. I was wrong, of course, and immediately investigated how the sense of calm and compassion, as well as academic rigour, had been achieved. The answer lay in the leadership: the skills of the headteacher, with her background in mental health settings, her two masters degrees and her teaching experience, had been strategically applied to create a compassionate culture. We videoed her every interaction with children, teachers, support staff, parents and workmen for a whole school day and, along with much discussion, were able to break those strategies down into something we could share with other educators. In this book, she shares her valuable experiences, insights and strategies, with powerful anecdotes.

The starting point

We looked at the 'reasons not to be cheerful' in the world at this moment, terrifying for many adults, let alone children:

- **Covid**
- **War between Russia and Ukraine and elsewhere**
- **Cost of living**
- **Parental anxiety and/or conflict**
- **Social media: negative messages, images, conspiracy theories, etc.**
- **Political fears**
- **Global warming**
- **Media doom and gloom: health, jobs, housing**
- **Learning difficulties**
- **Peer issues: bullying, cliques**

How these are manifested in schools will be very familiar to educators:

• **General anxiety** • **Body image issues** • **Stress on staff, fewer staff, less funding** • **Catastrophic thinking**	• **Bullying** • **Apathy** • **Exhaustion** • **Self-harming** • **Children feeling behind in class**	• **Social anxiety** • **Sexting** • **Fear/panicking** • **School refusers** • **Low self-esteem**

An integrated, practical approach

There appeared to be many 'bolt-on' strategies in place to solve the mental health epidemic, such as courses for teachers and support staff or meditation sessions for children, but we wanted, together, to explore ways in which we could present a fully integrated approach so that all educators in a school could influence not only the ethos of the school but also ways in which the content of the curriculum and individual lessons could be adapted. A summary of the parts and chapters now follows.

Summary of the content of the book

Part I: Why is everyone so anxious and what can we do about it?

Chapter 1 begins with insights into *why and how we have such an increase in mental health issues* in schools. This leads on to Chapter 2 with the two most significant theories for the ways in which we need to understand and help children: *projection and containment*. The scene is set for digging deeper and the practical strategies which follow.

Part II: Understanding and dealing with extreme behaviour

In this section, Angela Evans and Kate Moss tackle *the psychology behind extreme behaviour*, giving deep understanding to the actions of troubled and traumatized children, as well as clear strategies for dealing with these. Chapter 3 outlines crucial information about *attachment theory and attachment styles* then Chapter 4 examines emotional *and rational responses*. Chapters 5–7 uncover possible reasons for *anger outbursts, panic attacks, school refusers, self-harming and depression* and give comprehensive strategies for dealing with these within the school context.

Part III: Supporting the learning to reduce anxiety

This section deals with the *curriculum, content and organisation of learning and lessons*, linking throughout with how these strategies reduce anxiety. Chapter 8 uncovers pupil self-efficacy (their belief in their ability to achieve). Many structures and systems have been put in place in schools over the years which actually **lower** children's self-efficacy, so these are thoroughly explored. If you don't believe you can achieve you are bound to be anxious, let alone in the current climate, in which even young children these days are refusing to go to school or self-harming through their anxiety.

Chapter 9 deals with *effective learning partners* so that children are *continually supported in their talk and learning* by a range of both cognitive and social pairings.

The importance of knowing what they are learning is discussed in Chapter 10 and how learning intentions break down into clear success criteria *so that children know what they have to do to achieve and be successful*. Co-construction techniques make this even clearer, often analysing what good examples might look like. Without these elements, children do not know how their work will be judged, what they were learning and what success might look like: **all anxiety-ridden concerns.**

Cognitive science, in Chapter 11, has brought the concept of *easing the cognitive load* to the forefront of our minds, so this is also explored with tried and tested strategies for *helping children cope in a fast-moving, content-laden learning environment.*

Chapter 12 is focused on what feedback can be achieved during lessons rather than 'marking' after lessons and describes those *strategies which reduce the load for teachers as well as giving on the move feedback to children. Live feedback links powerfully with attachment theory, helping to reassure and contain our children.*

Moving on from frameworks for learning which reduce children's fear and anxiety, Chapter 13 is a goldmine of how *themes of anger, guilt, loss and so on can be integrated throughout the curriculum.* Topics are often covered with missed opportunities to explore difficult, emotional issues, so a comprehensive list of possibilities is outlined here, stemming from themes used in Clearwater School, common in many schools.

Chapters 14 and 15 focus on the fantastic opportunities to discuss emotions and reduce anxiety through the power of the arts. Chapter 14 explores *the potential of music, art, drama and nature,* then Chapter 15, through the amazing practice of Sarah Le Templier, looks at the close-up opportunities for *using powerful texts to explore with children difficult emotions and circumstances in our lives, while still focusing on academic learning intentions.* Examples are given, for instance, of tackling punctuation for speech through analysis of an excerpt from the book 'The Boy at the Back of the Class' concerning a refugee who joins a class and the dialogue that ensues between two of the characters. Letter writing is explored via the book 'The Iron Man' in which one of the characters finds it too difficult to engage with another character, so writes a letter expressing his feelings instead. The examples given are moving and powerful and exemplify the vital process of talk therapy.

Part IV: Creating a containing and compassionate school

Kate's valuable insights and strategies are outlined in this final part. She begins with Chapter 16 – *Vision and Values* – the steps taken to establish these with the staff. She then outlines *the role of a school leader* in Chapter 17. This is a perfect combination of theory and practice. She outlines, for instance, exactly how we might talk to *children 'sent' for misbehaviour* so that they take responsibility for their actions while still feeling cared for. She includes *raising teachers' self-efficacy, being a role model, creating trust and communication, perspective and resilience and community.*

This section and the whole book ends with Chapter 18 – **Looking after Yourself** – with theory and practice from Angela and Kate for the vital ingredient of all educators needing to look after their own mental health so that they can deal appropriately with the many challenges of teaching and continue to be a consistent and valued player in the harmony of a calm, caring and compassionate culture.

PART I

Why is everyone so anxious and what can we do about it?

1

The 21st century context

We're only human

Anxiety is a part of being human. Two hundred thousand years ago when *Homo sapiens* first evolved, we needed anxiety and stress to enable us to move quickly out of dangerous situations. We lived in a world with more immediate dangers all the time, which were soon resolved (e.g. avoiding a predator or finding food to eat). As we developed, we still had the same chemical composition in our brains but our anxieties became less immediate. Instead, we had generalised anxieties about work, food and keeping safe. We had the luxury of being able to appreciate each other's company and to develop art and music for our enjoyment. We had time to be curious about our immediate vicinity and to seek to be happy. By the 20th century, Maslow (1943, 1970, see Fig. 1.1) developed a hierarchy of our needs as individuals, which reflected our immense development as humans. In an imperfect world, however, we still hold on to anxiety and stress.

The technology revolution

In the 21st century, there has been a revolution that is already looking likely to have greater impact on the anxiety levels of humans than any other revolution humanity has undergone: the assimilation of technology into almost every aspect of our lives. It has allowed us to know what is going on not

DOI: 10.4324/9781003454434-3

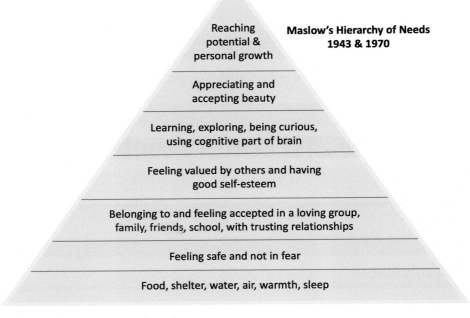

Figure 1.1 Maslow's hierarchy of needs

just in our local vicinity but in our entire world. This is positively transforming in the way we acquire knowledge, but it can impact negatively on our mental health. We now have an entire world to feel anxious about!

People who give us news are no longer town criers but companies worth billions whose interest it is to feed us news. We need to know what is going on in our world, but can we cope with it? We worry about climate change, wars, the growing population, to name just a few. The psychology behind social media and advertising is very sophisticated. We now need to manage algorithms that feed us more of what we already worry about.

Adults are generally more anxious and so are their children

Research from the Slee, Nazareth, Freemantle and Horsfall (2021) found that, in the last decade, anxiety and depression have increased, particularly amongst younger people and women. If adults are anxious, their children are too. Children soak up negativity. They are dependent for their survival on the adults who care for them, so they are finely attuned to their physical and emotional wellbeing. Anxious children can become depressed. It is tiring and debilitating to hold on to a sense of anxiety and uncertainty: it affects the body, the mind and our very being.

In 2021, Hickman et al published the first large-scale global survey on climate anxiety in 10,000 children and young people aged 16–25 years from 10 different countries around the world. They found that 59% of young people were extremely worried about climate change and 84% were moderately worried. Seventy-five per cent said they think the future is frightening, and 83% said they felt let down and betrayed by governments.

> Our findings suggest that climate change, climate anxiety and inadequate government response are all chronic stressors that could threaten the mental health and wellbeing of children and young people around the world.

Hickman et al. (2021)

An increasing amount of children in therapy are telling us that they don't want to have children and bring them into such a dangerous and difficult world due to their climate anxiety and fear of the future.

Those of us who work with children in the UK all know that mental health difficulties are increasing and have been for some time. In 2017, pre-pandemic, multiple agencies carried out a survey that showed an increase in emotional disorders in 5- to 15-year-old children in just 13 years (NHS Digital, 2017). Reasons were that parents were becoming increasingly stressed, exhausted and burnt out. We can add to this children's access to online sites, their exposure to celebrity culture, social media influences, their increased knowledge and feelings of helplessness around wars emerging in all parts of the world, a growing population and climate change.

In 2019, Sellers et al published their findings from longitudinal studies of different cohorts of children in the UK with **existing** mental health difficulties dating from the 1960s to the present day.

They concluded that child mental health difficulties have 'become more marked over time' and that this 'is a cause for major concern'. They point to our modern society as being less well-adapted today for promoting the healthy development of children with mental health difficulties.

The impact of the Covid pandemic on school staff: A UK school leader's perspective

Since the Covid pandemic, there has been a noticeable increase in the number of parents **reporting** anxiety both for themselves and for their children, with more requests for support. Alongside the societal pressures outlined above, this increase has also been attributed to the stresses and changes brought about by the pandemic. Little, however, has been recognised about the impact of the pandemic on school staff. We know there is a recruitment crisis in schools, and that supply agencies' vital pool of teaching and support staff is diminishing. So, what contributed to this?

Lack of guidance

For school staff, there was a mismatch between the public health guidance and what was being asked of them individually. The overriding message at this time was that people must remain at home, keep distance from everyone even family members as the danger to life was overwhelming. For teachers, however, this protection was removed.

Key messages from the government were delivered on the television before any guidance or information was received by schools from the Department of Education. This led to a concern of *Am I doing what I'm meant to be doing?* and *How, where and with whom can I check?*

Schools were not closed!

The media's view was that schools were closed. In reality, teachers were navigating a new and highly stressful situation. They were asked to support the emotional wellbeing of children and parents whilst also trying to process the situation on a personal level.

Staff had to very quickly become skilled in online teaching. A dual system of in-person (with key workers' children who were in school) and remote learning had to be devised. For those who bravely traversed the world of online teaching, this meant a real feeling of exposure, as parents could watch and judge. Add into this limited numbers of children allowed to mix, disinfecting everything on site and finding enough spaces for everyone to work safely whilst trying to keep children distanced from one another, is it any wonder anxiety was growing?

Whilst we, heard that social workers, educational psychologists, speech therapists and many other agencies would no longer come into schools or visit the home due to the danger to themselves, we, nevertheless, were expected to carry on. The responsibility, therefore, of spotting and managing safeguarding risks became difficult and worrying.

Teachers are not therapists

Parents then, and still now, turn to schools for support with an array of mental health needs for their children and for themselves, both within and beyond school. Resources within the wider community are stretched, and often it is staff within schools who are left to deal with complex and sensitive mental health issues that, in the past, would have been met by a dedicated mental health professional. This responsibility, on top of the already full-time occupation of educating children, can lead to teachers and support staff feeling unmoored and, at times, overwhelmed.

The fall out

Following this intense and unique experience, pressure on schools in England to 'deliver' has increased. Talk of 'Catch Up' somehow trivialised the experiences of the children and staff, as if there was a quick fix. Scrutiny both large and small continues, on every facet of school life, through Ofsted, Statutory Inspection of Anglican and Methodist Schools (SIAMS) and Governors and Parent View questionnaires. For those at the coal face, a very real worry emerges *Will I be the one publicly exposed as the weak link?*

To make it more difficult for schools, attendance nationally had plummeted: a direct result of many children and parents believing that being present in school was no longer a basic necessity.

> *Department for Education in England (DfE) published data for 12 December 2022 showed the absence rate for all schools nationally was 14.3%. This put the whole nation within the persistent absence category.*

The impact of the pandemic: Psychotherapist's perspective

In their meta-analysis (the bringing together of many studies about the same topic), Ying Sun et al (2023) compared mental health symptoms in the

general population across the world before and during the Covid-19 pandemic. They reviewed 137 studies with data from 134 cohorts. They found that changes in general mental health, including anxiety symptoms, from before to during the pandemic, had been minimal to small.

This research clearly tells us that the population, as a whole, was actually quite resilient during the pandemic and did not suffer noticeably from increased mental health symptoms. It became evident to many people working with children that, as the pandemic took its course, some children were benefitting from being at home with family, as they had opportunities to bond with parents and siblings.

Already anxious children in the UK

Most already anxious children, exposed to adults' worries and insecurities as a result of the pandemic, suffered from increased anxiety on top of their existing anxiety. Childhood Trust findings (2020), after interviewing 2,000 children with mental health issues, reported that 83% said the coronavirus outbreak had made their mental health worse. Many children who had improved and finished therapy with Dr Evans and her colleagues in England returned to therapy during lockdown as all their anxiety re-emerged, often in a more heightened state than previously.

Adults living and working with children have gradually had to take more notice of children's mental health difficulties over the last 50 years. During the last two decades, the increase in children who need help has sped up. Pre-pandemic, adults were already struggling to meet children's mental health needs, with too few staff and resources to go round. Since the pandemic, the increase has sped up even more but resources have remained the same.

Keep reading!

Yes, this chapter is hard hitting and depressing, but it sets the scene for what is to come and its importance. The remaining 17 chapters aim to give understanding and practical strategies to make the current situation more manageable, give actionable suggestions to teachers, support staff and school leaders and take schools and children to a more comforting, reassuring world of hope and happiness.

2

Projection and containment theory
The more we're contained, the less we project

What is projection?

If you hear the word projection, what do you think? If you are an artist, you might think of an image being reproduced on a screen through optical means; if you are a financier, you might think of a future projection for a rate of growth; if you are an actor, you might think of projecting your voice distinctly to an audience. All these definitions have something in common and might help us to understand the psychological definition of projection – they all involve something being moved from one place to the other. **The psychological definition means that a person *unconsciously* projects his or her emotions onto someone else.**

In understanding human relations, projection is an important process. It affects the way we relate to each other at quite subtle levels. Let's have a look at how we begin projections at an early age. We are all familiar with a little child having a tantrum. The child might scream, cry, stamp his feet and hit out at his carers. This is often accompanied by an angry, *I hate you, go away*. What is the child doing? The child who hits and shouts at his carers is projecting his anger onto them. It is quite unconscious. The child isn't tactically thinking about how he can hurt them. **He is simply overwhelmed with negative emotions, which he**

DOI: 10.4324/9781003454434-4

Figure 2.1 Projection

has to split off from the rest of his emotions and project them out onto others (Fig. 2.1).

Being on the receiving end of projection

Have you ever been in the position of the carer with the child having a tantrum? How does it make you feel? Tense? Stressed? Angry? If so, the child has successfully projected his feelings onto you. As the child begins to calm down, you are left feeling irritated and upset.

As we grow, we learn to hold onto our feelings and to deal with them, but we still find it hard at times to manage them. Have you ever been in a discussion or argument with anyone who is becoming heated and upset? How annoying is it if that person tells you to calm down when it is obvious that they are the stressed one? It makes you feel immediately stressed. That person has successfully projected their feeling of stress onto you as they tell you to calm down. Consciously, they see themselves as a calm person. They don't want to admit to their stressed nature. So, unconsciously they project it onto you.

> *Projection is an unconscious process. When overwhelmed with emotions, when unable to face our negative feelings, we project. Someone else carries it instead of us and we feel better.*

Why do we project?

Freud (1895) first became aware of projection as outlined in Gay's (1995) biographic work. He describes it as **unconsciously expelling negative or harmful feelings or wishes that are too unacceptable to us, onto others**. As a Jew himself, Freud became painfully aware of anti-Semites transferring what he called their own 'low' or 'dirty' feelings towards Jewish people, then 'detecting' those feelings in the Jewish person. We are all horribly aware of such projections today.

Later theorists developed Freud's insight and saw projection as a defence against anxiety. 'Low' and 'dirty' feelings, or as we might word it today, negative and harmful feelings, can make us feel anxious about ourselves and who we are. Add to this our anxieties about our external world as well as our internal world. In Chapter 1, we referred to all the reasons we might feel anxious: exhaustion, burn out, poverty, social media influences, wars emerging, a growing population and climate change. These can give us emotions we find uncomfortable and overwhelming. Our anxiety can become so huge that we have to unconsciously put these uncomfortable emotions into someone else.

> *I'm doing fine and managing my life but my partner is driving me mad! She's so anxious all the time and well over the top about global warming. There's something wrong with her.*

Our current understanding of projection is seen as an unconscious way of relieving our unwanted emotions and of relieving our anxiety, which can take several forms. We might argue with our partner when we get home after a stressful day when things didn't go as we thought they would. We might get cross about the way they load the dishwasher when we're really furious about the new policy that just came into our school. We might also project our own wishes onto others and become disappointed when they cannot live up to them.

Projection in schools

In schools, children who are stressed, fearful, anxious or traumatised can project extreme feelings onto peers. Educators are familiar with parents who tell them their child isn't happy at school because of certain disruptive children in their class. Challenging children can affect a whole class. It is important that adults in schools are aware of what is happening and can help a class of children by talking about emotions. This enables the class to understand that some children need extra help and attention in many different ways. Additionally, adults need to provide extra support for children who project.

Bullying

Bullying is a form of projection. When trying to help and understand bullies, as children or adults, Freud's insight is just as current as it was over 100 years ago. The bully often bullies because inside s/he feels insecure, unlovable and nasty. It is easier to project these uncomfortable feelings into others, thus relieving him/herself of intolerable emotions. In turn, a victim can become overwhelmed by the bullying, lose self-esteem, become angry and feel unlovable. The victim then feels just like the bully; when this happens, the victim is in projective identification with the bully. Ultimately, this technique of relieving oneself of intolerable emotions doesn't work. The bully needs to keep bullying; if s/he stops for too long, the bad emotions return. So, the bullying gets worse. When children get into this cycle, adults are vitally needed to help the bully and the victim to think about their feelings and to make them feel safe in the knowledge that feelings can be tolerated, however bad they are.

The following table gives common signs that bullying is or could be happening and suggested action points.

Signs of bullying	Action
Overt physical or verbal harm to a peer/s	Before attempting any conflict resolution, talk and listen to the bully/ies and the victim/s separately. Give consequences to the bully/ies after talking as a result of what has been found out.

Signs of bullying	Action
Hidden physical or verbal harm to a peer/s	All educators in school to notice and be interested in peer relationships, especially with children who are struggling to separate from parents/carers at school drop off and children who are showing signs of unhappiness at school. All educators to liaise with each other, with a central person, e.g. SENDCo, gathering facts. Vital to liaise with and listen to parents/carers, even if you believe they are being over anxious. They know their child/ren best.
Isolating a peer/s by turning others against them	As above but particularly notice children who play alone. They might prefer to be alone, but they might be suffering from being isolated.
Children hiding in cloakrooms, classrooms or hidden places in playgrounds	Be diligent and ensure adults on playground duty look and listen and involve themselves with children. An available adult is a child's safety point. Adults are not available if they are talking intently together whilst on playground duty.
Children leading games, clubs and hobbies	Bullies are vulnerable and insecure. Some children who lead are natural leaders and manage it well, but others lead due to their insecurities. Note how the leader leads. Do they manage their emotions whilst leading or become controlling and upset? Look and listen to them, especially in the playground. An allocated adult to talk and listen to them if you suspect they are leading due to their insecurities.

Projecting onto staff

Children in schools can also project extreme feelings into teaching staff, who can feel angry, frustrated, anxious and even traumatised after a child has massively disrupted a lesson with an aggressive outburst or hurt another child. So, we see this unconscious projection going through the school, a bit like a ripple from a pebble when you throw it into the water, and it can, in extreme circumstances, go as far as the local authority (Fig. 2.2).

Special Educational Needs and Disabilities Coordinators (SENDCos) are the people who will particularly receive projections from children and from staff, as they are the staff members who represent the most challenging children. SENDCos whom Dr Evans worked with for her doctoral research experienced feelings of rejection, anger, uncertainty and abandonment from colleagues, let alone from the children with whom they worked. One of the

Figure 2.2 Projections ripple outward through the system

signs that this was happening was how they projected into Dr Evans, the outsider coming in to support the SENDCos, as in the following anecdote.

Anecdote

Mia, the SENDCo, was 15 minutes late for our appointment. She took me to her room, then, without explanation, left me for another 10 minutes. I felt very abandoned. Mia returned and told me about an incident in the playground where her school leader had left her to deal with it alone. She had turned to a colleague, come to collect me, then returned to her colleague. Mia had successfully projected abandonment into me. In our next session, we talked about it and Mia could own how upset she had felt about being abandoned by her school leaders.

What is containment?

Let's revisit the little child having a tantrum, projecting into his parents, saying he hates them and wishes they would go away (Fig 2.3). A good enough parent, despite feeling stressed, tense and angry, will hold on to their emotions and will help the child to feel calmer. They might hold the child, distract and tell the child it's OK and they still love them. **They'll be calm themselves or they'll stand back from the situation until the child is over the tantrum. This is containment.**

Figure 2.3 Containment

Bion (1962) developed the theory of containment, where the mother's capacity to act as a container for the infant's projections, to make sense of them, to transform them and to return them to the infant in a more thought about and acceptable form contains the infant's anxiety and regulates the extreme emotions.

In a 'normal' loving family, it can be hard to contain a screaming infant, but most of us manage it most of the time. If we think of the challenging children in our schools who may hold unbearable feelings, for all sorts of reasons, we can begin to understand how some children might need extra therapeutic help from all the adults around them to have their angry, negative emotions contained. The power of the destructive impulses of some traumatised children and young people is so great that they need a network of containing adults around them, containing not just the children but also each other.

> In therapy, the therapist acts as a container for what we daren't let out, because it is so scary, or what lets itself out every so often, and lays waste to our lives

Winterson (2011)

Figure 2.4 Containment ripples inward through the system

Containment in schools

For challenging children, containment is a vital function of schools. It is also vital for all children and adults to have good enough experiences of containment. We all need containment, whoever we are, and especially so in the context of increased anxiety in the population.

In a containing school, instead of the ripple of projection going from the children through the adults in the school, containment reverses that ripple (Fig 2.4). Containment needs to happen throughout all organisations, with the leader of those organisations being contained too.

If a school leader is feeling contained, they will be able to contain other adults in the school, from teaching staff to maintenance staff to parents. They will also be able to contain the children in the school. If a class teacher is feeling contained, they'll manage to contain a child's projections much more easily than if they weren't feeling contained themselves. They'll be able to nip them in the bud, leading to the classroom being a safer place emotionally so children can learn more easily.

The more we're contained, the less we project – let's listen to our emotions

In order to achieve this, we all need to apply what the good enough parent does. A good enough educator will be aware of their emotions, especially in the midst of an incident. They might feel anxious, scared, having a racing heart, angry and frustrated but will resist projecting these feelings onto the other person, whether child or adult. They will hold onto them while they model calm and clear leadership. When the encounter is over, as soon as possible the educator needs to think about the emotions that were projected into them, to make sense of them and to process them so they feel better.

This sounds all very well, but, in the life of a busy teacher, it may also sound unachievable. We can all become stressed by our time limitations, so it is often a matter of changing thought patterns and behaviour. For example, educators could make it a part of their communication to 'check in' with each other in the staff room. This doesn't take extra time but perhaps a conversation over tea that might become an unfixable and negative conversation could instead turn into something more positive. An imagined example:

Oh my god, Gemma is so difficult today. I don't know what to do with her. It's not fair on the others, she's so disruptive. I can't wait to get a new class next year; we just can't learn properly.

Wow, that she really difficult this morning?

Yes, she actually attacked Ahmed for taking her pencil. She stabbed his hand with her pen.

Oh my goodness, that must have made you feel dreadful.

It really did. I felt like attacking her but of course I didn't. I was angry though.

I would have been too. Brilliant you hung onto your anger. That's a tough thing to do.

Thanks. Yes, it was hard. And I didn't sleep well last night either.

Poor you. We've got to look after each other in this job.

Yeah. (Looking pensive)

What did you do? How did you deal with it?

Jane looked after Ahmed and luckily his hand was OK but it's recorded. I managed to talk to Gemma about why she was so angry at the beginning of break.

You're amazing. I'm taking notes! Hope you get a better sleep tonight.

Thanks. Thanks for the chat. (Smiles)

Note in the example that the containing teacher doesn't comment on her colleague's outburst about the class not being able to learn properly. Neither does she comment on her wish to have a new class and get rid of

The more we are contained, the less we project

Figure 2.5 Containment

Gemma. The containing teacher is focused on her colleague's feelings. She says, *That sounds really hard. That must have made you feel dreadful.* By doing this, she gives space for her colleague to talk about her anger. She gives her empathy and contains her feeling of wishing to escape, finally offering her genuine praise for the way she deals with Gemma, Ahmed and with herself.

We all naturally want to reassure and problem solve when people reach out to us. If we can hold those impulses, really listen to each other's emotions and be genuinely interested in each other's wellbeing, it creates more open and trusting relationships. We all need this in order to feel contained. It helps to create a whole school culture of containment and wellbeing. Some people are more naturally able to contain others, but if it is in the culture of the school, it emanates out to all educators, and projections from adults and children will be reduced (Fig 2.5).

A whole school culture of containment and wellbeing

In schools that provide containment for every person in the school community, projections of distress, fear and anger are received and thought about, from senior managers through to the child. When the world seems to be a frightening place and mental health is on the rise, we need it even more. The following conditions provide a starting point for creating such a culture, a list of ideas on how to begin to create such a culture. These conditions are fully explored in *Part IV: Creating a Containing and Compassionate School.*

Conditions for a whole school culture of containment

- **Trust** and **openness** between all staff
- **Open doors**
- Being **available** for parents wherever possible
- Schools are **communities**: encouraging active parental involvement
- Being creative with **break times**
- Considering children who are overwhelmed in **large gatherings**
- **Connecting** with children and with each other
- **Modelling happiness: smiles** trigger hormonal changes helping neurons connect
- Being **genuine** and **interested** in the child and colleagues – even when hard
- **Listening** attentively
- **Thanking** children for sharing with you
- Having positive **body language**
- Being **consistent**

Positive school experiences build resilience

A classroom culture of containment and wellbeing

Within the context of a containing school culture, a teacher can create a containing classroom culture. In fact a teacher can create a containing class culture whichever school they're in, but it is easier if there is a whole school approach. The conditions which follow should help teachers to start thinking about it. As with the containing school culture, it is a list to develop and make your own.

Conditions for a classroom culture of containment

- **Create a structured and predictable routine** in the classroom
- **Make the** classroom safe, with no potential 'weapons'

- Create a **calm** corner in the classroom
- Speak **quietly, calmly and lovingly**
- Encourage children to **share worries** with teacher and friends – worry/chat box
- Create a culture of talking in the classroom where children can **share emotions, opinions and worries**
- Give a message that **all emotions are valuable and** acceptable – name different kinds of emotions so they are understood whenever the opportunity arises

If children are contained, not only do they project less but also they learn more. It reduces their anxiety. Children who come into school with their fight, flight, freeze responses aroused can experience a reduction in their arousal if they feel safe and held within a loving school community. This enables them to more easily switch on the cognitive part of their brain, the 'thinking brain', thus enabling them to listen and take in information and to work with it.

Educators are vital to the culture of containment

In schools, above all, all educators need to be supported and contained, both for their own health and wellbeing and for that of the children they work with. You are really important to this culture of containment. Your ability to not just teach but to act as containers for the children depends on you having good enough emotional wellbeing and feeling contained yourselves. You are vital to turning the mental health of a school around by looking after yourselves.

> *Teachers are not – nor should they be – therapists, but their relationships with the children they teach have enormous reparative as well as developmental potential.*
>
> *Youell (2006)*

PART II

Understanding and dealing with extreme behaviour

3

Attachment styles in the primary school context

In this chapter, Angela takes us through the significance of attachment theory and how it has a direct link with the role of the educators in a school and especially in identifying and understanding extreme behaviours. She first explains 1) why knowing about this is important, then 2) summarises the theory and finally 3) shows what we can do in schools for each of the main attachment styles, to reduce anxiety for all involved.

Why do we need to know about attachment theory?

No child is born alone. They are born within the context of a parental relationship. This parental relationship, with one or two parents, is their first attachment relationship. It forms the basis of future relationships. Many children are lucky enough to have secure attachments. Some children have to leave their first parent/s and form attachments with new parents/carers. Most manage to remain with their parents of birth.

After the parents, the class teacher is one of the first people with whom the child forms an attachment relationship. Teaching assistants and other staff in the school are also a part of becoming secure attachment figures for the child in school. You, the educator, are a vital part of forming a growing child's relationship to the world. The child can extend their secure

DOI: 10.4324/9781003454434-6

attachment with their parent to you, the educator. If they have not been able to form a secure attachment with parents, you are someone with whom they can experience their first secure attachment. **That is truly special and is the main reason you need to know about attachment theory.** It helps you to think about your relationship with the children in your class/school and to live it. You will also be able to understand the link between children's early relationships and their behaviour, which impacts directly on their learning. Geddes (2006) pointed to the immense potential of schools to replicate a 'secure' experience for children in their school. A whole school staff can create a culture where each student can experience a reliable and 'secure base'.

Do I have any securely attached children in my school?

A securely attached child is one to be envied. Below are the behaviours associated with secure attachments:

- Explores, experiments and learns through play
- When older, can make sense of own and others' feelings
- Good self-efficacy
- Self-confident
- Trusts others and asks for help
- Manages stress and frustration
- Is empathic
- Can resolve conflicts

You might be able to think of children in your school who approach these behaviours, but they will not be able to maintain them all the time because they are human and life isn't always simple, even for a relatively securely attached child.

Word of warning for you, the educator

Learning about attachment theory can make us question our own childhoods and those of our children. Before you feel failed or a failure, please note that there is no such thing as a completely securely attached person! Our attachment styles are on a spectrum and often overlap. Attachment theory is simply a useful guide to help us in our work with children.

Attachment theory – a brief introduction

John Bowlby (1944), a psychologist, psychiatrist and psychoanalyst, was the founder of attachment theory. He began to see in his work a direct link between early emotional deprivation and later behaviour. He saw the importance of a 'secure base' for an infant. You may be familiar with the sight of toddlers taking their first exploratory steps. They will glance back regularly to check on their parents, their 'secure base'.

Survival!

Bowlby (1969) saw that we develop attachment behaviours in order to ensure our survival. That is why infant animals, including humans, are so adorable and irresistible. We want to look after them! Babies develop all sorts of behaviours that attract us to them – they smile, they reach out and they laugh. They are saying,

> Please look after me. I'm completely dependent on you so I need you and so far, you're pretty nice so I'll keep reaching out to you.

Sadly, some parents cannot adequately look after their infants, which then threatens their survival, so those infants might adopt other behaviours – they might not reach out for fear of upsetting an adult, they might look away and they might cry a lot in order to get noticed. They are saying,

> Please look after me. I'm completely dependent on you so I need you but so far, I'm not entirely sure that you'll feed me and look after me when I cry too much or even smile too much and I keep getting it wrong but I'll do my best to keep you close and keep me safe.

Patricia Crittenden (2015), a clinical psychologist who studied under Mary Ainsworth from 1978 to 1983, developed a model of attachment that is more complex than the categories of attachment would suggest. She emphasised our need for survival and how we organise our attachment behaviours around it.

Links between children's early relationships and their behaviour

Bowlby's most notable early paper was *Forty-Four Juvenile Thieves*, which he first published in 1944. He researched the family histories of delinquent children who were stealing and compared them to a control group who were not. The findings of significant links between early separation from parents and delinquency led him to research further. Later he was joined by Mary Main and Mary Ainsworth who developed his ideas. Ainsworth, Blehar, Waters and Wall in 1978 developed the Strange Situation, where infants are observed in a safe room with toys and a kind adult to see how they behave when their mother leaves the room for a few minutes then returns. We can see from the table of Strange Situation findings that the researchers saw differences between how different infants responded.

The Strange Situation		
20-minute laboratory test One-year-old child 2 separations, max 3 minutes, benign stranger		Ainsworth, Blehar, Waters and Wall (1978)
A: Secure	**B: Anxious /Ambivalent**	**C: Avoidant**
Less ready to explore Close to mother on return	Wary of stranger Upset by separations Clingy on return	Not upset Maintains exploring behaviour Avoids mother on return

They saw the **secure** infant as one who showed signs of losing their secure base when their mother left the room and were pleased to see her return.

The other two infants were seen as having **insecure** attachments. The anxious/ambivalent infant was more noticeably upset at mother's absence than the secure infant and clingy on her return. The avoidant infant was avoidant of mother on her return and seemingly not upset.

These findings led to the beginning of formulating attachment styles. The first formulations were **secure** and **insecure,** which initially consisted of avoidant and anxious/ambivalent styles. More were to follow. The most significant style for understanding troubled children was the insecure *disorganised/ controlling/traumatised style of attachment identified by Main and Solomon (1986).*

How would the disorganised/controlling/traumatised infant have behaved in the Strange Situation?

A disorganised attachment style is so called because the infant can find no organised way of staying safe. They cannot seek for more attention, they cannot withdraw, they cannot smile extra hard and when under two years old they cannot even run. This is because they cannot predict what the parent will do next. Thus, their behaviour and reactions to stay safe are a disorganised array of pathological responses triggered by the fight/flight/freeze response. Patricia Crittenden referred to this disorganised attachment style as a child organising its behaviour around unpredictable adult behaviour. Worded this way, the 'blame' lies less with the child – they are simply doing their best to survive in impossible circumstances.

D: Disorganised/controlling/traumatised		
Freeze	Fight	Flight

In the Strange Situation study would have behaved in one of the following ways:

- A freeze response – not looking at anyone, not playing, sitting entirely still.
- A fight response – taken full control of the situation by throwing a toy and crying loudly.
- A flight response – crawling or toddling towards the door or the other side of the room, not looking at either adult.

This behaviour would have started on entering the room and seeing the presence of a stranger, even a benign and friendly one. It would have remained the same whether the mother was present or absent.

Behaviours of insecurely attached children

Many of us are lucky enough to experience good enough parenting, which is not perfect but which puts us somewhere in the secure category of attachment. Others are not so lucky due to inherited factors, family circumstances and environments. They then fall somewhere in the **insecure** category of attachment. Parents are not always intentional in their parenting styles. Their children evoke all sorts of emotions from their own childhoods, which can be overwhelming and can lead to repetitive patterns of negative parenting.

How can I use this theory in my school?

For the purpose of applying attachment theory to the primary school, we will focus on the three main types of **insecure** attachment behaviours that have arisen from the research:

a) **Resistant/ambivalent/anxious attachment style** (upset by separation, wary of strangers and clingy on return of mother).

b) **Avoidant attachment style** (not upset by separation and avoids mother on return).

c) **Disorganised/controlling/traumatised attachment style** (would adopt fight/flight or freeze responses).

Insecure – resistant/ambivalent/anxious attachment style

These children might be:	
• Anxious • Tense • Irritable • Reactive • Clingy/over-dependent • Angry • Attention-seeking	• Bullying • In enmeshed & entangled relationships • Oscillating between loving and hating • Escalating confrontation to get attention • Easily distracted

This attachment behaviour has three names because it incorporates three related aspects of behaviour. A parent who is resistant to meeting their child's needs is likely to feel ambivalent about them. They will be anxious about how they feel. These messages of resistance, ambivalence and anxiety will be given to the child in many verbal and non-verbal ways. Children pick up very easily how their significant adult feels about them. Such parents/carers tend to have weak boundaries and a lack of confidence about their parental control.

The anxiously attached child in the classroom is the one who may cling to the teacher and always seek adult attention. That is how they have learnt to get noticed. They have experienced a parent/carer who is ambivalent about their existence, sometimes wanting them and at other times pushing them away. They are uncertain that their attachment needs will be met, so they exaggerate their needs to ensure they will be met. Anxiously attached children can be tense and irritable. They are the children who will become caught up in dramatic peer relationships.

These children need:
• Letting them know they're in your mind through regular direct one-to-one interaction • Clear boundaries

- Short, timed, independent tasks
- Structured friendship activities
- Consistent and reliable adult support
- Responsibility for tasks within a learning group, where they can be involved with others but also experience some independence
- Transitional objects from the adult – 'Can you look after this for me please?'
- A curriculum that incorporates issues such as separation and independence (see Chapters 13, 14 and 15)

Insecure – avoidant attachment style

These children might be:	
• Needy but distant • Isolated • Having subtle displays of anger • Blaming of others • Bullying • Unaffectionate	• Emotionally self-sufficient • Self-reliant and independent • Showing low self-worth • In denial of distress • Undemanding

The avoidant parent is one who struggles with displaying or even feeling emotions. They will ignore the child who is expressing upsetting emotions such as anger, sadness, anxiety or jealousy. It is much more comfortable for them to have a sensible, measured child who can manage their emotional life independently. They will offer their child what they need in a practical way but won't necessarily be too interested in them for fear of engaging too deeply.

The avoidant child in the classroom is the child who is often unnoticed or even forgotten. They have learnt to blend in, to accommodate others, to keep their emotions hidden. They may even appear to have little affect and are not always the children who make adults smile. Their self-esteem is generally low, and they are unlikely to ask for adult help.

These children need you to:
• Let them know they're in your mind through regular indirect interaction • Focus on the task more than on the relationship – sitting alongside sooner than face to face

- Give task-related praise
- Give measured interpersonal contact
- Make sure you notice the avoidant child and maintain a presence
- Help with transitions as change promotes a sense of anxiety that adults will withdraw
- Facilitate a curriculum that incorporates issues such as expressing all emotions, hidden or dangerous feelings, closeness and distance (see Chapters 13, 14 and 15)

Insecure — disorganised/controlling/traumatised attachment style

Freeze Fight Flight	These children might be:
• Underachieving • Anxious • Very controlling • Over-reactive • Over-sensitive • Depressed • Switched off • Violently angry • Anxiously dependent	• Unable to understand, distinguish, control emotions in self or others • Experiencing strong feelings which are overwhelming

As previously described, the disorganised/controlling/traumatised infant can find no organised way of staying safe. They cannot seek for more attention, they cannot withdraw, they cannot smile extra hard and when under two years old they cannot even run. Thus, their behaviour and reactions to stay safe are a disorganised array of pathological responses triggered by the fight/flight/freeze response. Parents of children with this attachment style are generally traumatised and suffering from disorganised attachment styles themselves. They can be very controlling towards their children. Most children who are unable to live with their birth parents and/or have suffered developmental trauma have a disorganised/controlling/traumatised attachment style. It is an extreme attachment style and one that often needs an entire network of adults.

These children need:
• Let them know they're in your mind through frequent, direct one-to-one interaction • One to one time essential • A network of adults around the child • Absolute clarity about rules • Structured activities in class and break times • Help with all transitions as can be a trigger for an outburst • Make the child feel **safe** • A curriculum that incorporates issues such as how to keep safe, managing big feelings and dangerous feelings
The child attacks because s/he feels threatened

Kate's experiences of the various attachment styles:

Our classrooms are a melting pot of children's attachment styles. It can be hard to respond to the need behind the behaviour when faced with a sullen, sulky child, a needy demanding one or a child who 'kicks off' angrily with the smallest provocation. I have been privileged to work with some exceptionally skilled teachers who have replicated some of the missing early childhood experiences through seemingly small actions. Whilst these in themselves will not immediately change a child's behaviour, they will allow trust to build and provide evidence to the child that they are worthwhile.

Insecure – resistant/ambivalent/anxious attachment style

These are the children who become your shadow. Those who, for example, appear by your side when you are on playground duty and are limpet like in their efforts to remain with you. Unlike the children who have a chat and move on, the insecurely anxiously attached child wants only your attention and is very resistant to leaving your side. This limpet-like quality happens in the classroom too. In my experience, teachers are very skilled at providing meaningful jobs for children like this and supporting them with peer relationships.

Insecure – avoidant attachment style

I am always concerned when a child does not ask for help. I don't mean the embarrassment of not knowing an answer, rather a child that is so completely self-reliant that they do not ask for assistance under any circumstance at all. These children often present as sullen in the classroom, especially if there is too much notice of them. I have in mind a child that was very much like this. This

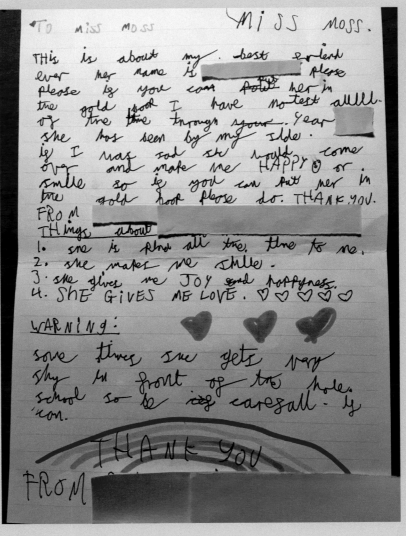

Figure 3.1 Letter to Kate

child would often be mean to other children. The meanness to others was pointed but cleverly hidden, and, when faced with evidence of a misdemeanour, the child would lie or blame others. The facial expression was emotionless and sometimes defiant. Within all of this though, it was clear that the child was deeply unhappy. The child gave the appearance of not caring about school work, but this masked an inability to seek support. If an adult praised the child for specific work or smiled warmly, it would be rebuffed not through words but through body language and an almost dismissive 'blink and you've missed it' sneer. This child was highlighted through pupil progress meetings as a 'focus child' and appropriate support matched to need undertaken. Over a very long time, small changes were observed. The child began to express sorrow and amazingly also started to appreciate the kindness of others.

One child in the class sent me a letter asking for the child in question to be put in the Gold Book. The letter can be seen in Fig. 3.1 with its transcript below.

To Miss Moss

This is about my best friend ever her name is ...... please please if you can put her in the Gold Book I have noticed all of the time through Year...she has been by my side. If I was sad she would come over and make me Happy ☺ or smile so if you can put her in the Gold Book please do. THANK YOU.

Things about ....

    1   **She is kind all the time to me**
    2   **She makes me smile**
    3   **She gives me JOY and happiness**
    4   **SHE GIVES ME LOVE**

WARNING:

Sometimes she gets very shy in front of the whole school so be careful if you can.

THANK YOU

FROM

....

Insecure – disorganised/controlling/traumatised attachment style

A colleague of mine impressed me hugely with her compassionate response to child in her class. This teacher moved her 'desk' next to a child who was suffering from regular angry outbursts. Not only was this child angry but they were also hypersensitive to perceived slights from peers and wanted control. They presented as angry, wary and exhausted. In response to these behaviours, the teacher moved her papers and notes onto the child's table and would begin each lesson from there. She would then circulate around the class and return to the spot next to the child. This, although she was unaware of it, recreated the secure attachment that the child was craving. The brilliance of it was that the teacher did it quietly and with warmth. There was no big announcement; she just knew intuitively that this child required her to provide a secure base. She recognised that the child was unable to ask for what they needed and deep down felt unloved and unlovely. Her visible presence was a tangible sign to the child that they were likable. Up until this point, the response that the child had experienced to their volatile, angry behaviour had been the complete opposite of this – people wanting to move away and children not wanting to be friends. Whilst much emotional work was still required, the teacher provided a vital message to this child that 'you are wanted in my classroom'. Over time the child began to trust this teacher, the bond was strong and the child sought the teacher out in times of distress and anger.

Knowing about attachment theory and how it can be seen in children's actions is so helpful in teaching. I first came across the attached table (Figs. 3.2 and 3.3) when I was a Special Educational Needs and Disabilities Coordinator (SENDCo). It looks at attachment styles and how they may play out in the classroom, whilst the table was devised to support those children who have been adopted or are looked after, it is a valuable tool for any child with an attachment need. https://www.swindon.gov.uk/download/downloads/id/6470/ attachment_behaviours_and_what_you_might_do.pdf

A knowledge of attachment theory really does help us understand our children better and create an environment that supports their development rather than working against it. It highlights how any classroom strategies that develop self-efficacy, problem solving and accepting and learning from mistakes will also benefit our anxious, needy, controlling pupils, as these strategies scaffold and offer support in an acceptable way without singling out the child. They are 'normal' classroom practice and available to all.

Behaviour management across the classroom - Gloucestershire Adoption Service
What behaviours can result from attachment issues and what might you do?

adopt!

Attachment type	Behaviour	What this means for the child	Possible triggers	What might you do?
AVOIDANT (I'm OK, you're not OK)	Withdrawn – unable to make or keep friends / Bullies other vulnerable children	I have to rely on myself and nobody else. I respond to frightening situations by fleeing. I don't expect other people to like me. I pretend to be strong by making other children do what I want.		Introduce a buddy system. Consider 'circle of friends' approach. Encourage the child to help around the school.
	Refusal of help with work	I was left helpless before. I'm not going to be left helpless again!	Singled out for 1:1 support.	Encourage work in pairs or small groups. Ask the child to help another who is less able.
	Loses or destroys property	I have no sense of the value of anything. I have little interest in things if they are not mine. I am angry and I take it out on things.		Validate the child's feelings, "I can see that you are angry..." Help the child repair/restore where possible – together.
AMBIVALENT (I'm not OK, you're OK)	Talks all the time, asking trivial questions	I feel safer if I do all the talking. I want to communicate but don't know how.		Have set routine. Make sure all first tasks are simple and achievable. Seat child close to you. Allow child to wait quietly.
	Demanding teacher attention all the time	I fear that if I don't let you know I'm here you may leave me on my own. Even negative attention is good. I fear getting it wrong.		Notice the child explicitly. Give child something to look after for a while. Give child responsibilities for things (not people).
	Hostile when frustrated	I will feel shame and humiliation if my difficulties are exposed.	Task that is hard/new/unusual.	Small step differentiation. Use timer to divide tasks.
	Poor concentration, fidgeting, turning round	I must scan the room all the time for danger. I must stay hyperaroused. I dare not relax.	Sights, smells and sounds can trigger panic as reminders of past trauma.	Arrange seating so there is no one behind the child but where you can stay in contact. Laugh with the child, even at silly things.
	Refuses to engage with work	Getting things wrong is frightening. Being wrong will lead to rejection AGAIN.	Task that is hard/new/unusual.	Make sure both are acceptable and accessible! Make lessons/tasks very structured (use multiple choice/closed questions). All materials to hand.
DISORGANISED (I'm not OK, you're not OK)	Tries to create chaos and mayhem	It feels chaotic inside so it feels safer if it is chaos outside.		Focus on modifying most serious behaviour. Validate the child's feelings. "I can see that you are angry/upset..."
	Oppositional and defiant	I need to stay in control so things won't hurt me. I do not want to be exposed as stupid. You are horrible like all adults.	Task that is hard/new/unusual.	Be assertive but keep emotional temperature down. Avoid showing anger, irritation or fear. Start each day with clean slate.
	Sexually aggressive	I know from past experience that sex = power and I want to be in control.	Variety of stimuli including stress.	Record all incidences very clearly. Seek advice from other agencies (see back of the information guide).

Gloucestershire
COUNTY COUNCIL

Figure 3.2 Gloucestershire behaviour management grid 1

Attachment type	Behaviour	What this means for the child	Possible triggers	What might you do?
	Unable to accept praise or to have fun	I am not worthy of praise and you are stupid if you don't realise how bad I am. I am unlovable.		Do praise but don't be too effusive and be specific about what you are praising. Praising the child privately may be more acceptable to them.
	Physically or verbally abusive	I respond to frightening or threatening situations by fighting, fleeing or freezing.		Avoid threat of removal or rejection. 'Time in' not 'time out.' If unavoidable, do so positively "I need to get on with the class – you come and sit here till you feel better." Speculate aloud why it might have happened (don't ask child to explain).
	Ignores instructions	I have too much anxiety to be able to listen. I can only retain one instruction at a time as too much going round in my head. I am easily distracted.		Keep format same each day. Describe plan of activities for session at outset. Do the child's remembering for him/her! Let the child make lists on post-its.
INDICATORS OF ATTACHMENT DIFFICULTIES GENERALLY	Sulkiness, avoids eye contact	I don't dare see what others think. I have no words to describe my feelings – looking sulky is a cover-up.	Face-to-face contact. Being told "look at me when I'm talking to you".	Find ways to reassure - smile, thumbs up. Encourage playing games to make children laugh. Sit side by side.
	In trouble at break times	I fear rejection by my peers. I panic in crowds. I cannot self-regulate when stressed.	Unstructured time.	Reduce time in playground, introduce tighter structure and supervision, create inside 'retreat', establish nurture group.
	Lying or living in fantasy	I prefer to make things up how I would like them to be. I'm not sure who I am or what the truth is. I don't know the difference between fantasy and reality.		Avoid accusing child of lying or fantasising. State the truth of the matter briefly and simply.
	Stealing	I have no expectation of getting something so I'll just take it. I have no idea you may feel hurt or anger and when I see the effect I feel powerful.	Rejection by peers.	Do not insist on 'sorry'. Suggest an action that might repair damaged relationships. Try not to leave desirable things lying around!
	Behaviour suddenly deteriorates	There is a painful anniversary coming up. A new sibling has arrived; have got contact with birth family coming up/ have just come from contact with birth family.	Special occasions like Christmas, birthdays or Mother's Day, before and after weekends.	Be sensitive in curriculum delivery. Allow child time and space to manage feelings away from the classroom.

Figure 3.3 Gloucestershire behaviour management grid 2

Gloucestershire
COUNTY COUNCIL

School as a secure base

As Geddes (2006) pointed out nearly 20 years ago, within a containing and compassionate school, a situation of safety and security can be replicated for a child. Schools are about so much more than learning. They are about providing the fertile ground from which learning can happen. For children who have had little or no experience of secure parenting, schools are places where they can learn first-hand about relationships that promote wellbeing and reduce anxiety.

> *Dr Evans and her colleagues have worked with fostered children in schools where the teaching staff were the people the children had known the longest in their lives. These vital adults were the most secure attachment figures they had. They provided a secure base, from which the children could begin to relax and explore their world.*

The Graduated Pathway or Multi-Tiered System of Support (MTSS)

Before we dive into the next chapter, dealing with extreme behaviour in classrooms, it is important that we first address a crucial support structure: *The Graduated Pathway or Multi-Tiered System of Support (MTSS)*.

As teachers, our core purpose is the education of our pupils academically, socially and emotionally. Most pupils in mainstream education are able to access the high-quality provision provided by their teacher and progress moves forward as we would expect. For some pupils, additional support may be necessary. Approaches that follow recognised research-based interventions are essential in this process. Best practice is to follow a defined Graduated Pathway.

In essence, this means a structured approach with agreed levels of support and adherence to agreed key components.

- ◆ Level/Tier 1 high quality teaching in all areas: academic, social and emotional
- ◆ Level/Tier 2 additional support in a small group: targeted academic, mental health and/or behaviour support
- ◆ Level/Tier 3 intense instruction following an individualised plan: targeted academic, mental health and/or behaviour support. This can be in house or specialist support

The key components within each level are familiar to teachers, that of assess, plan, do and review. This review cycle is a key factor to ensure our actions are having a positive impact, that time is not wasted on ineffective support and progress is maximised. For the graduated pathway to be successful, an appropriate evidence-based programme must be followed within a clear, agreed time-frame: the use of precision teaching to close particular phonic gaps, for example, *or a programme that addresses social and emotional development such as Thrive (www.thriveapproach.com)*. All adults must be invested in problem solving, in careful evaluation of the data, in communicating and working with other agencies when necessary. The infrastructure must be in place to support this process led by a committed senior team.

This knowledge and suggested strategies that follow will support you in your everyday teaching and in moments of crises. It will strengthen your knowledge as a practitioner in discussions with colleagues, your wider senior leadership team and external agencies when creating individual education plans, but most of all it will help to create a compassionate and containing learning environment day to day.

4

Emotional and rational responses

Values as the foundation of a compassionate school culture

The following chapters, dealing with the various types of extreme behaviour, need to be read in the context of the whole school culture, focusing especially on the established vision and values of the school.

The agreed, much discussed values for Clearwater School can be seen on page 48. They form the basis of every conversation, every decision and every thought about how the staff want children and adults to be treated: **with love, care and compassion.**

In Part IV, *Creating a containing and compassionate school,* the last section of the book, Kate outlines how she organized and led the creation of her school's vision and the journey to determine these core values with the staff.

Understanding ourselves first

A key aspect of primary school life is having to deal with children's extreme behaviour. Reasons for their behaviour are often complex and hard to understand, so understanding the difference between emotional and rational responses and how to monitor and control our responses is critical if we are to create a fair and contained culture.

DOI: 10.4324/9781003454434-7

Clearwater Academy Values		
RESPECT	RESPONSIBILITY	JOY
COMPASSION	COURAGE	COMMUNITY

Am I emotional or rational or do I just freeze?

Most of the time we are not aware of whether we are operating in a mainly rational or mainly emotional way, as we tend to see our responses as just these: responses, with thoughts and feelings attached. However, the more we understand about our fight, flight, freeze instincts, the more we can understand our own reactions and learn to manage them in helpful ways. You might be wondering why we would need to: I am sure we've all experienced a situation where we've responded in a way we didn't mean or found we couldn't respond at all.

Have you ever had that awful, tongue-tied moment, when the words just won't come? Only to find that when you're at home later you have 101 witty retorts you wish you'd thought of in the moment ....

Our survival instinct takes over and emotions become extreme

Those tongue-tied moments are times when our survival instinct has taken over, the brain blocking our rational thought and seizing control in order to protect us. This is often explored in trauma training of how to support children in schools. What is often not acknowledged though is that this survival response is operational in us all the time, not just at times of obvious stress or crisis but often in our day-to-day reactions. For most of the time this does not cause us any difficulties: the two co-exist happily, but, as we become more tired, one part, and it can be either the emotional or rational, can take over in a bid to protect us. This is our survival instinct in action. Both the emotional and rational parts are necessary and of importance – one is not better than the other. Often, in modern society, our survival response can be activated when the threat is not at the level of life or death it was designed for. It is, therefore, helpful to be able to recognise our own patterns of behaviour so that we can learn to maximise the parts we want and reduce those we don't. This takes conscious practise.

How to balance my thinking and feeling – notice, recognise and refine

When we operate solely on our emotions, we can often see things in black and white, with a stark contrast between what we see as right or wrong.

This can lead us into more conflict than is necessary and, at its worst, leads us to dig our heels in to a particular viewpoint. We then look for evidence to back up that viewpoint and might not be invested or interested in understanding a counter argument.

The **PETI** (Practise, Effort, Time, Input) model used for effective learning (see page 92) can be helpful for us as a scaffold to learn about ourselves and our more fixed viewpoints. For example:

a) finding out some more information about the impact of different ways of responding (input) and

b) looking to apply this information to ourselves (effort) will pay dividends.

Each person is different and will have specifics that relate solely to them and their prior experiences, so what I'm describing is a broad brush. If you take the time to **notice, recognise and refine** your responses, you will find that your emotional and rational sides will work in harmony and the threat response lessen, thus reducing your stress. This then leaves space for us to feel more settled and enjoy aspects of our work that might previously have caused unspecified anxiety.

Notice, recognise and refine **in action**
The scenario
How many times have you heard a colleague (or you yourself might have done this) comment on a parent in quite damning terms? Commonplace are comments about a particular aspect of parenting: a parent's lack of willingness to read with a child, for instance?

The teacher often then looks for other 'signs' to back up their view of the poor parenting, heaping other perceived slights and faults on this person. If the parent is late, or the child is tired, this all contributes to the teacher's original 'correct' viewpoint and unforgiving judgement of 'poor' parenting.

The impact
The end result of this judgement is that we ourselves feel stressed. We blame the parent for the child's lack of progress, the threat here being the increase in teacher workload in order to meet our performance-related target. It might also be due to a particular personal belief (e.g. that education is important or that part of a parent's job is to read with their child). We

might have made an assumption that this is the 'right' way and everyone will of course agree with us. Leaving this unexamined has the potential to continually wind us up internally, as we worry away at the wrongness of the situation, at the harm this parent is doing to their child by 'not reading with them' and whilst nothing has actually changed, we may find ourselves ever more uptight and cross.

A balanced approach

A more rational response would be to seek to understand the situation, to find out the background to the situation and to acknowledge that this parent might not hold the same perspective as us. When we operate rationally, we're able to appreciate the grey areas. Is the parent actually causing harm or are we just annoyed as we have to find a way to bridge the gap of no consolidation at home? If we acknowledge that 'life is not perfect', it becomes easier to accept that this parent is unable or unwilling, for reasons unknown to us, to read with their child. We can deal with the consequences of this without it causing spikes in our emotional equilibrium.

The example I have used is deliberately not at the extreme end of what we as teachers deal with. It illustrates that if we can master our day-to-day responses over the little things, we will then be able to manage our stress/ threat response more effectively when we are faced with larger issues, such as the anger and powerlessness we might feel when dealing with serious safeguarding difficulties and/or extreme behaviour in the classroom.

Applying our understanding when dealing with extreme pupil behaviour

Let's take a closer look at those larger issues, the ones that flick our survival instinct straight into operation. We're definitely struggling to be rational at those times and our emotions are not grey but more extreme, black and white with a large amount of red alert thrown in too. It is at times like these that we can draw on our capacity to hold on to noticing and refining our emotions. We can keep in mind two learnt and practised questions:

- ◆ *Question 1: How am I feeling?*
- ◆ *Question 2: Is my feeling stopping me being rational?*

It needs a little time and input to remember this in times of stress, but the more you practise, the easier it gets:

- ◆ *Question 1: How am I feeling?*
- ◆ **Answer 1: Angry/Scared/Powerless**

- ◆ *Question 2: Is my feeling stopping me being rational?*
- ◆ **Answer 2: Yes – My anger is quite big/I feel a bit scared and tongue tied/I'm not sure what to do.**
- ◆ **Answer 2: No – I am angry/scared/powerless but I'm aware of it enough to remember not to make assumptions, to keep thinking and questioning my motives.**

Once we can understand and name our emotions, for ourselves and for the children in our care, we have much more likelihood of being able to deal with the issues. If, for example, someone is flexing their muscles, verbally or physically, they are often scared. If you can recognise that and name it, our emotions become less extreme, red alerts go down and we can start to think again. A balance of emotional and rational is restored.

What children need

Children generally need a little more help than most adults. Children need your non-verbal, observing self. They need your full attention, which you can give once you locate why that strong emotion is coming up in you and who it really belongs to. Children's brains are not sufficiently mature enough to notice, recognise and refine their responses. They need to see adults modelling how to do it, and they need to have emotions named, gently and slowly. We all know that if you tell an angry child they are angry, they will reply, 'No, I'm not!' and they will just feel more angry. But if the adult says, 'There are some big feelings here' it is much more neutral. The feelings are put between you both and aren't located in any one person. Then, we can look at the feelings without feeling ashamed or attacked.

Appropriate responses

So, once you have your answer to whether you feel balanced or not, you can begin to deal with the issue of what to say to the child: *There are some big feelings here. Pause. It's OK. Pause. Let's sit over here. There's a lot of anger going on/These feelings can feel scary/It's hard to know what to do, isn't it?*

As stated, our emotional and rational parts are both necessary. Children are often more driven by their emotions than by their logic; they have less developed reasoning capacities than adults. It is therefore helpful to follow their emotional narrative and not to get stuck in their rationality or lack of it! When a child is trying hard to tell us about their hurt feelings in response to something that happened at break time, it can be easy for us to adopt a rational narrative instead of listening to their emotions. We might ask questions like:

Why were you all huddling in the corner?

What exactly did you say?

You couldn't have been in the green zone because that's for Years 5 and 6. Do you mean the red zone?

Those questions might be useful but they can come later, once you have heard the emotional narrative. The child who is feeling hurt can feel attacked by rational questions, which can be experienced as the last straw. There is a chance they can make the child's communication with you shut down. Comments rather than questions are more helpful in the immediate telling of the story. Some comments might be:

That sounds really hard.

You must have felt upset.

Goodness, I can hear that Daisy was upset too.

Once the child feels that their emotions have been heard and acknowledged, they are much more likely to be able to engage their thinking brain.

Let's imagine a typical scenario: a fight in the playground and how it might have been dealt with. There follows an analysis of the teacher's responses, both emotional and rational, both of which are necessary but managed.

Anecdote

A class teacher speaks to two children who were fighting in the playground. They have had a chance to calm down. The teacher, though, is feeling angry with the child who seemed to instigate the fight. She clearly saw him kick the girl standing next to him. She is aware that the boy, Aaron, is bigger than the girl, Chantelle, who had retaliated with a smack to his face, but he had grabbed her hand and pushed her down before a teaching assistant (TA) on duty had stopped the fight. The teacher knows that Aaron's family struggle and the father is addicted to alcohol, which has impacted on the children, often resulting in disruptive and aggressive behaviour.

Initially the teacher speaks to Chantelle. She tells Chantelle that she saw Aaron kick her and asks the girl if anything had happened to make him do that. Chantelle shakes her head, looking very sorry for herself. The teacher gives her a lot of sympathy and assures her she will be speaking with Aaron.

When the teacher speaks with Aaron, she tells him that he used his bigger size against Chantelle, which was unfair, and she points out that he made the first move. Aaron stares into space, as if unmoved. She tells him he needs to apologise to Chantelle straight away. Aaron continues to stare, but he begins to bite his lip hard, holding onto his emotions. The teacher commands him to look at her; he brushes his hand against his eyes, still looking away. This action prompts the teacher to remember to ask Aaron if anything had happened to make him kick Chantelle. When she asks him, Aaron softly replies, 'She called my dad a loser and said she saw him eating out of a bin'. The tears begin to fall. She says to him, 'You must have been furious'. He nods. She apologises to Aaron for not asking him that question before.

After more investigating with both children, Chantelle admits her provoking comment. The teacher, in speaking with each child, can then talk about how hard she had found it to ask the right questions as she had felt angry with Aaron. She talks to how hard it can be to think when there are big feelings around. She talks to how much words can hurt, as much as kicks, and how neither of those things are allowed. She invites Chantelle and Aaron to find solutions with her that will help to resolve the situation.

Analysis of the teacher's emotional and rational responses

What happens here? We've all been in situations where we hold some pre-conceived ideas about children and their parents in our schools. Aaron is a disruptive boy so carries a reputation with him. It would be perfectly reasonable for the teacher to assume that he initiated the fight for no apparent reason but perhaps because he had had a difficult morning at home before coming into school that day. And any teacher would feel angry at witnessing what happened. Let's just examine the scenario again as it emerged.

Anecdote: with analysis

A class teacher speaks to two children who were fighting in the playground. They have had a chance to calm down. The teacher, though, is feeling angry with the child who seemed to instigate the fight. She clearly saw him kick the girl standing next to him. She is aware that the boy, Aaron, is bigger than the girl, Chantelle, who had retaliated with a smack to his face but he had grabbed her hand and pushed her down before a TA on duty had stopped the fight. The teacher knows that Aaron's family struggle and the father is addicted to alcohol which has impacted on the children, often resulting in disruptive and aggressive behaviour. We know so far that the teacher does have a pre-conceived view of Aaron based on the school's experience of him. The teacher has also answered Question 1 – she knows that she is feeling angry.

Initially the teacher speaks to Chantelle. She tells Chantelle that she saw Aaron kick her and asks the girl if anything had happened to make him do that. Chantelle shakes her head, looking very sorry for herself. The teacher gives her a lot of sympathy and assures her she will be speaking with Aaron.

The teacher already knows she is angry but she hasn't yet answered Question 2 – is my feeling stopping me being rational? She is also holding an unconscious anger about a boy hitting a girl, which touches a little on her own history. We all hold values and we are all triggered by different issues, which can make it hard when we are trying to hold on to our rational selves amidst strong emotions.

When the teacher speaks with Aaron, she tries to curtail her anger but can hear that her tone of voice is a little sharper with him than with Chantelle. *She tells Aaron that he used his bigger size against Chantelle, which was unfair, and she points out that he made the first move. Aaron stares into space, as if unmoved.* This ignoring behaviour is a further trigger for the teacher. *She tells him he needs to apologise to Chantelle straight away. Aaron continues to stare, but he begins to bite his lip hard, holding onto his emotions. The teacher commands him to look at her; he brushes his hand against his eyes, still looking away.* It is the brushing of his hand against his eyes that moves the teacher to notice how she has stopped thinking clearly.

At this point, it is the vulnerability of Aaron that moves the teacher to consider his emotions. She realises that she didn't ask Aaron if anything had happened to make him kick Chantelle. She had asked Chantelle but not Aaron.

When the teacher asks Aaron if anything had happened to make him kick Chantelle, he softly replies, 'She called my dad a loser and said she saw him eating out of a bin'. The tears begin to fall. The teacher now realises Aaron's anger. *She says to him, 'You must have been furious'. He nods.* The teacher also realises that she hadn't checked in with Question 2 – is my feeling stopping me being rational? She had tried hard to remain aware of her anger but now sees that, despite her efforts, it had stopped her from asking Aaron the same vital question she had asked Chantelle – Had anything happened to make Aaron kick Chantelle? *She apologises to Aaron for not asking him that question before.*

After more investigating with both children, Chantelle admits her provoking comment. The teacher, in speaking with each child, can then talk about how hard she had found it to ask the right questions as she had felt angry with Aaron. She talks to how hard it can be to think when there are big feelings around. She talks to how much words can hurt, as much as kicks, and how neither of those things are allowed. She invites Chantelle and Aaron to find solutions with her that will help to resolve the situation.

The teacher has learnt so much from this exercise and puts it beautifully into practice. It is not too late to make good what happened. In fact, it is a perfect example to the children of how human we are and of how marvellous mistakes can be in informing our ways of relating to each other.

5

Anger outbursts and panic attacks

Figure 5.1 The traumatised child projecting anger.

DOI: 10.4324/9781003454434-8

Anger

What is anger?

Anger is an intense emotion, which can be accompanied by physical symptoms such as a racing heart, feeling hot and sweaty, having tense muscles or a churning stomach. It is a powerful emotion which people tend to feel so strongly that anger 'bursts' out of them. The anger outburst is generally strongly experienced by everyone around them too. This is a classic projection, as described in Chapter 2: *Projection and Containment Theory*.

At the opposite end of the scale, some people struggle to express anger. They might have learnt to suppress it over the years, partly due to character and perhaps due to having witnessed or experienced frightening anger outbursts in the past. Instead of having an anger outburst, their anger will sit with them, gnawing away at them, at times feeling like it is growing inside them. It is still as intense and powerful even if it is not expressed and can cause mental and emotional distress if it is not acknowledged and released.

So, anger doesn't have to be an outburst and it doesn't have to be suppressed. It can be acknowledged, talked about, felt deeply, understood and then released. This is called processing the emotion. When we are children, we tend to have anger outbursts, as our brains are not developed enough for us to regulate our emotions. As we grow older, we learn to process our emotions. A developed adult will mostly be able to avoid an anger outburst or a suppression of anger and instead will be able to be assertive in their communication of their anger. Thought of in this way, we can see anger as a useful emotion that can be transformative if adequately communicated. It is an intense emotion that can cause great harm and lead to verbal or physical violence, or it can help to change the way people think and can build nations. It was Nelson Mandela's righteous anger about the extreme racial prejudice black people were suffering in South Africa under the apartheid system that led to him becoming an activist and harnessing and channelling his anger into positive peaceful protest (rather than violent action) through his speeches and the civil rights movement.

> Great anger and violence can never build a nation.

Nelson Mandela (1990/2012)

The angry child

Babies are not born with the ability to regulate their emotions. It develops over time and experience, alongside all the other skills. As educators, we help children to regulate their emotions by building their emotional intelligence. We name emotions with them, we model how to respect and care for others and we encourage co-operation.

Most children learn how to manage their emotions. However, children who have had adverse experiences, children with disorganised, traumatised attachment styles and/or highly anxious children can still struggle with their emotions, especially with anger (see Fig. 5.1). They may have regular anger outbursts that seem to come out of nowhere. These children need our special attention and love, even though they are the ones who disrupt our lessons, make us feel stressed and impact on the rest of the class.

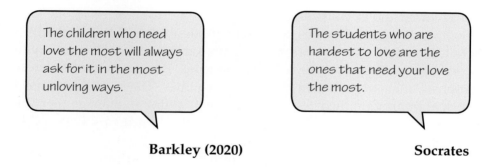

The children who need love the most will always ask for it in the most unloving ways.

Barkley (2020)

The students who are hardest to love are the ones that need your love the most.

Socrates

They are the ones who will likely be suffering at home, who will have an accumulation of negative emotions, anxieties and experiences. One 'straw on the camel's back' triggers the outburst. It is too much for the child to bear, so they unconsciously split it off and project it outwards.

What happens to the adult's brain when a child has an anger outburst?

The adult who is in charge of a class of children when a child throws a chair across a room into the midst of other children will have a series of reactions, all happening in a split second. The adult may experience feeling hot, sweaty, a racing heart, tense muscles and a churning stomach, identical to some of the angry child's possible experiences. They may feel frightened, angry, dismayed and likely a combination of all three. Both child and adult are in a fight, flight, freeze mode, driven by the amygdala sending signals to the hypothalamus, which stimulates the autonomic nervous system and triggers the release of adrenalin and cortisol, allowing us to deal with a threat promptly. When this happens, our prefrontal cortex, which is the centre of executive function, shuts down as we need all our energy to deal with the threat. The prefrontal cortex enables us to stay focused and complete tasks. It is our thinking brain and just when we need it the most, it cuts out.

The adult's challenge

It is therefore a huge challenge to the adult to acknowledge what is happening not just in the room but in themselves. They need to acknowledge their response in their thoughts and feelings, to take control of it and to contain it. Then they can meet the child's emotions with calm. In the midst of their outburst, the child will be quite unconsciously aware of the adult's reactions and of the way the adult contains their responses. This in itself will calm the child. It conveys the message that the adults are in charge, can regulate their emotions and can create safety. Moreover, it reduces anxiety in the children and in yourself.

So how do we achieve this seemingly impossible task? It is really difficult to take control of one's extreme responses and emotions. It comes with practice and requires a degree of self-knowledge. Educators need to know themselves, their triggers and their vulnerabilities. They will likely need to work at improving their responses and their ability to manage them by discussing with colleagues, by being able to reflect on themselves and to learn with each new experience.

In Dr Evans' experience, it is a continual journey of self-discovery. It can involve some painful self-reflection, as seen in the following excerpt. For an educator, it needs to be a part of their continuous professional development, alongside the many other necessary skills.

Anecdote

I was working with an extremely disturbed boy, Jason, who couldn't manage mainstream school. As part of my assessment, I visited him in his school for children with emotional and behavioural difficulties. The visit started well. I observed him in the playground, in a heightened state but managing to play with friends. I was aware that my presence made him especially 'wound up' and excited.

When it was time to go into class, Jason refused to move. He stayed in the corridor then ran back into the hall, throwing himself on the stage with a huge crash. I watched helplessly as two members of staff skilfully placed themselves either side of him, stopping him running further and preventing him from hurting himself. Jason screamed, writhed, cursed, bit, threatened and finally gave in. My emotions were going through the roof. I tried to stay calm but inwardly felt horrified at the suddenness of the rage Jason was experiencing. The staff either side of him seemed so assured and almost relaxed. I was aware of managing to control my body, but I felt that fear and horror must be written all over my face. I felt really traumatised, helpless and foolish.

I didn't take this to supervision until a few weeks later. In retrospect I was too defensive and shamed. Jason had projected his unbearable emotions deeply into me. Yet when I did talk about the incident, I was aware of my body shaking as I told the story. It is only now in writing this that I realise how inadequately I processed the experience. The powerful projection remained in my body, causing unnecessary stress. I had felt too guilty in my role as observer, somehow to blame for Jason's behaviour, and it had stopped me from taking care of myself.

The practicalities

Once this reflection process has begun, the practicalities of what to do when a child has an anger outburst become much easier. The most challenging aspect is **managing your emotions so the children can manage theirs**:

What happens, in order	What to do
A child has an outburst of anger, either physical or verbal, alone, in a small group or in the classroom.	Let the outburst happen. The child will not be responsive to reason. Keep the child and others safe. Have two adults readily available at all times. Have an open-door policy in classrooms.
As the adult, you become aware of overwhelming emotions and/or physical symptoms.	Note your symptoms and emotions, hold them, breathe and meet the child's emotions and behaviour with calm. Use Q. 1 and Q. 2 from the previous chapter: *How am I feeling? Is my feeling stopping me being rational?*
The child begins to calm down.	Help the child to breathe, to take their mind elsewhere and take them for a walk. Young children still need help to regulate their emotions.

What happens, in order	What to do
Normality is restored.	The educator needs to self-reflect on what happened to them or to speak with a colleague. Process your emotions.
	Educator to speak and listen to the child who had the outburst, to help them to reflect on the event and to think about what they can learn from it. Take care not to induce shame. Note your tone of voice and non-verbal messages as you interact with them. Have you adequately processed your own emotions?
	The educator needs to attend to other children who might have been affected, to reassure them and to help them to understand what happened.
	The educator to speak with parents/carers and to listen to them with compassion and respect.

Note that the teacher/teaching assistant need to look after themselves, to take care of their own emotional health by seeking support, by talking to colleagues. Seeking support shows strength. It reflects an ability to acknowledge the importance of containing strong projections not just in children but in ourselves.

> *The more we're contained, the less we project, and the more we can reduce anxiety in our schools.*

Panic attacks

What is a panic attack?

A panic attack is actually an intense experience of anxiety. It is generally sudden and overwhelming in its onset. The most noticeable symptoms are physical. They include heart palpitations, sweating, shaking, shortness of breath, numbness. A panic attack can last just a few minutes or can be much longer. The person is generally very frightened by the symptoms. They feel like they are losing control of their body, and there is a sense of impending doom. A typical response will be *'I had a panic attack. I thought I was going to die. I just couldn't breathe'.*

It is for this reason that, where breathing deeply needs to happen at the end of an anger outburst, it needs to happen at the beginning of a panic attack. The adult needs to breathe with the child and stay completely calm, even though they may be panicking inside. Unless the child has a medical condition, they will be able to get enough breath in.

Anecdote

Sama, the Teaching Assistant, suddenly noticed Maryam looking very pale and shaking. There seemed to be no apparent reason. Sama asked Maryam what was wrong. 'I can't breathe', Maryam replied, looking terrified. Her breaths were deep intakes followed by no in breaths at all, then another deep one. Sama felt frightened too. She instinctively sat next to Maryam and began to breathe, regularly and evenly. Between breaths she said, 'It's OK', 'nice and slow', 'I'm with you'. As she did this, she watched Maryam carefully, thinking she would send a child to the main classroom for the Class Teacher. After a couple of minutes, Maryam began to regulate her breathing to match Sama's. Sama reassured the other children around her. She inwardly sighed. The worst was over.

The following suggestions for dealing with a panic attack and what happens after, as with anger outbursts, include the most challenging part: the emotions experienced by the adult. Sama had to hold on to her own fear and model calm, all the time thinking of Maryam's safety and the other children's wellbeing. She managed her emotions so Maryam could manage hers. After the event, she spoke to the class teacher and relayed her fears while the panic attack was happening.

What happens, in order	What to do
A child has a panic attack, where they look pale, breathe fast, tell you they can't breathe, might say they think they're going to die.	Try to move the child into a quiet space if possible. Have two adults readily available at all times. Have an open-door policy in classrooms.

What happens, in order	What to do
As the adult, you become aware of overwhelming emotions and/or physical symptoms.	Note your symptoms and emotions, hold them, breathe and meet the child's emotions and behaviour with calm. Begin to breathe with the child, regulating their breath, speaking between breaths with calming phrases like, 'I'm here', 'It's OK', 'You're doing great'. This reduces anxiety, fear and makes the child feel safe.
The child begins to calm down.	Ensure the child has five or ten minutes to recover from the panic attack before returning to the classroom. Stay with them.
Normality is restored.	The educator needs to self-reflect on what happened to them or to speak with a colleague. Process your emotions.
	Educator to speak and listen to the child who had the panic attack, to help them to reflect on the event and to think about what they can learn from it. Take care not to re-trigger the fear. Keep your voice light so you convey a message of not having been frightened yourself by the panic attack. Have you adequately processed your own emotions?
	The educator needs to attend to other children who might have been affected, to reassure them, to help them to understand what happened.
	The educator to speak with parents/carers and to listen to them with compassion and respect.

6

School refusers

There is emerging new terminology for this very recent phenomenon, but in this chapter, we are using the term 'school refusers', as we believe its meaning is known amongst educators.

Keeping the whole picture in mind

When children are referred to me, the therapist, for school refusal, I think of two things – the place and people they are refusing to leave and the place and people they are refusing to go to.

Once I've met with parents/carers, I get a good idea of what's involved with those two aspects of the problem. I then communicate with someone at the school – class teacher, Special Educational Needs and Disabilities Coordinator (SENDCo) and in reality it is often whoever I can manage to find who has time to speak to me. Once this pre-therapy work has taken place, I really know what to focus on. Yet still surprises come my way.

The child may bring issues that the adults didn't even know about. There may be intense worries about people at home or at school that the child has never shared. That's where I need to get to work:

DOI: 10.4324/9781003454434-9

> *I need to:*
>
> **Listen, communicate, liaise, contain, gently challenge, reassure, look at my own emotions that are being aroused, try not to take sides, keep the whole picture in mind, take care of other people's emotions.**

We'll come back to how all of us can achieve all or some of the above later on in the chapter. First let's look at the 'why'. Why do children refuse school?

What makes a child refuse school?

Reasons for school refusal are many and complex. Some of the reasons are given below.

Separation anxiety

There might be a poorly or vulnerable adult at home who the child doesn't want to leave. The child could feel in some way responsible for them. The child could also in reality be a young carer. Families can hide their home situations due to concerns about children being removed. In this situation, the child would rightly feel anxious about leaving a vulnerable person to care for themselves.

Sometimes if a parent suffers from letting their beloved baby grow and go out into the bigger world, afraid of what they might encounter, the child picks up on this same fear of the world and doesn't want to leave the parent. With children who don't live with their birth parents, the dynamics become more complicated. These children are likely to have a disorganised/traumatised attachment style and an internal view of the world as being frightening. They may not want to leave the familiarity and safety of home.

Generalised anxiety

Symptoms of anxiety manifest in different ways in different children and are on a continuum. This makes it harder to spot if a child is not good at showing their emotions and isn't suffering acutely. Some children can hold

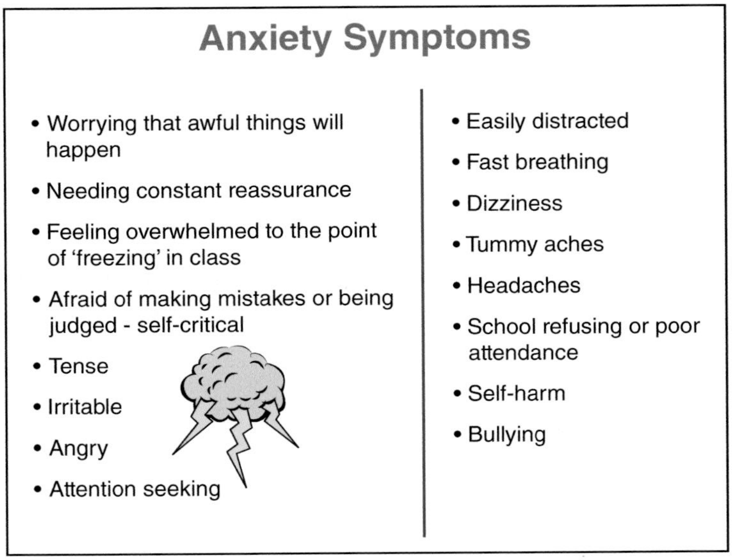

Figure 6.1 Anxiety symptoms

anxiety at school for years and go unnoticed until they feel they can't manage to hold it any more. That's the point at which they might refuse to go to school. It can appear to come out of nowhere. Have a look at the symptoms in Fig. 6.1 and consider whether children in your class/school might be suffering with anxiety.

Bullying

Bullying at school must always be considered when looking at school refusal. It can take place in very subtle ways, at times by the children we would least expect to bully. Ongoing comments that put a child down and constant marginalising of a child can impact their self-esteem, cause them huge misery and lead to school refusal. In Chapter 2, we talked about bullying being a form of projection. The bully often bullies because inside s/he feels insecure, unlovable, perhaps overwhelmed by negative feelings. It is easier to project these uncomfortable feelings into others, thus temporarily relieving him/herself of intolerable emotions. A repetitive bullying cycle develops when the insecurity returns, with bully and victim both locked in.

The learning environment

The learning environment also plays a huge part. Education derives from the Latin word 'educare', meaning to nourish, to bring up, to mould, to bring forth, to lead out. It is no small task to be an educator. You are responsible for not just bringing a child information but also for nourishing a child's self-efficacy, for leading them out into the world. Learning is an exciting adventure but, as with all adventures, it comes with many challenges. Children can fall through the net at many steps along the way, and in primary education, they will still be too afraid to challenge what their trusted educators say and do.

Formative assessment is hugely important in helping children to have positive experiences of learning. It structures learning so that children understand what they are doing and are not afraid to question or to make mistakes. They experience happy and positive learning environments cognitively, emotionally and socially, with such practices as random talk partners, task-related praise, learning for the love of learning, having clear learning intentions, co-constructed success criteria, knowing what good ones look like and in-the-moment feedback.

Nonetheless, even with these in place, some children can feel so worried or anxious about not managing to access their learning or about being bored or embarrassed because they are not being challenged adequately, their strategy is to refuse to attend school altogether. Children's individual needs should be picked up as early as possible so that they can experience the interventions they deserve.

What can the educator do?

The educator is vital to helping school refusers. With the right interventions, therapy is not needed. Let's break down the 'I need to' list from the first section of this chapter. What can the educator do to help with cases of school refusal?

Strategies
• Meet with the parents/carers, listen, contain, challenge where necessary, reassure, take care of the parents/carers' emotions • Speak to the child, listen to them, communicate with them, let them know they are in your mind, encourage them to share worries, reassure them the adults can help with problems • Liaise between adults and children, bullies and victims, see people individually, bring them together as needed

- Put strategies in place, such as individual timetables, reduced school hours, being met at the school gate, learning from home, slowly building towards a full return to school
- **Look at your own emotions**

You might already do most of the above. Some of the listed tasks belong not just to the class teacher or teaching assistant but to the SENDCo or other school leaders. You need to work as a team to manage school refusal because of the variable, sensitive and complex dynamics involved.

The containing educator has more chance of reducing anxiety and school refusal

Let's focus on the hardest task – looking at your own emotions. Children who refuse school can cause frustration and annoyance in the adults around them. Educators can be really helpful in enabling a parent/carer to feel heard and understood. In order to do this, they need to not just listen but also to hold onto their own possible feelings of frustration and annoyance. They need to accept what the parents/carers bring them. They can feed back to the adults what they are saying. They can acknowledge how frustrating it must feel for them. And while doing this, educators must hold on to their own emotions and not let them spill out. This is containing. If educators can contain parents and carers, they are less likely to struggle with school refusers. This is because if parents/carers feel contained, their children feel contained. This will reduce anxiety and nip bullying in the bud. School will be experienced by the child as a safe place as they will know that the adults in their life are talking, helping to create safe learning environments for them.

As stated throughout this book, in order to do this, educators need to know themselves, their triggers and their vulnerabilities. They will likely need to work at improving their responses and their ability to manage them by discussing with colleagues, by being able to reflect on themselves and to learn with each new experience.

When to seek outside help – the team around the child

At times, if school refusal cannot be helped with the above interventions, the graduated pathway approach (see page 45) suggests that other agencies need to be contacted and a wider team around the child needs to be formed. This in itself makes the child, the parents/carers and the educators feel held and thought about and contained. It shouldn't make anyone feel judged and if they do experience this, it needs to be addressed. Being on side with parents/carers is vital to reduce their own potential feelings of isolation and shame.

Two anecdotes by Kate now follow from her experiences of school refusal. Her insightful analysis of these then follow. In the first, the child had been brought to school but refused to go inside. In the second, a more common occurrence, the child is refusing to leave home to go to school.

Anecdote 1

A new child was due to begin at our school. I met the parent briefly prior to the start date and had many phone calls. This gave me valuable information about how, for the child's own safety, a change of residence was required. I was informed that the child's behaviour had become volatile. This situation also brought into the child's life a raft of unknown professionals.

The parent drove to the school on the appointed day. The child refused to leave the car. The child screamed loudly that they were not coming in. The parent came inside the building to fetch me. I went out to the car and introduced myself; I said that I understood this must seem very strange, being at a different school. I explained that the parent was fulfilling a legal duty in bringing them to school rather than being unkind as it was clear that they wanted to stay with their parent.

Removed shoes made it very clear that they were not going to budge. I offered the child a choice – they could stay in the car and I would bring the work to them, or they could come in.

I then spoke to the parent and said that I expected the child would like some time to make their decision. I thought it would be quite cold waiting in the car and so would they like a coffee brought out?

I then made a coffee and brought it out to the car. The child at this point said they were going to stay in the car. I suggested that they bring the cup back to the office when they were ready and returned inside school saying I would just go and sort out the work to be brought out.

Very shortly after the parent and child brought the cup to the office. I then asked the child if they would like to see the classroom.

Whilst the child was outside, I primed the teaching staff so they were ready with warm smiles.

The child was still incredibly reluctant, walking at a snail's pace down the corridor, at times stopping completely. Once at the classroom, the child could not *manage to go in and so sat with their parent in an adjoining room. A member of staff brought some books and slowly shared the book with the child and parent. The adult had put a soft toy cat close by that is quite lifelike and purrs when stroked and gave this to the child to hold whilst looking at books. At this point, the parent explained to the child that they had a commitment elsewhere and would return to collect the child later.*

Over the next few weeks, variations of this situation occurred. I would often receive a phone call stating that the child was having a 'melt down' at home and refusing to put on shoes or get dressed. The approach was always the same, to give time and encourage the child over the threshold. The parent did sometimes have to carry the child into school and leave an extremely distressed child with me and another member of staff. The child would scream and shout, although stopped short of throwing or breaking anything. I would sit on the floor with books, and quietly read, engaging in a reading 'tag team' with the other adult. We would discuss the book in very quiet voices, turning the page slowly, pointing to what we liked and our favourite passages. Gradually, the child would calm down and join in with the discussion. Then, the slow process of moving from the room to the classroom would begin.

This was not a linear process: there were days with steps forward and backwards, but the approach was always the same. Eventually, the child felt able to enter the classroom and began to settle.

Anecdote 2

This child had been at the school since reception. I received a phone call saying that the child was crying, refusing to get dressed and saying that they felt ill. The parent did not think they were ill and was unsure where this behaviour was coming from. The parent said that they were going to give the child some TLC (tender loving care) and they would be at school the following day.

On the following day, the child said the same thing, so the parent decided to ask a grandparent to help bring the child to school. The child came to school very upset and was helped into school by a family member.

The next day the child, whilst still teary, came into school without support.

It became apparent that the behaviour followed a pattern. It would recede for a week or two and then a repeat episode would appear, with the child point blank refusing to get dressed or come to school. When the child became distressed, it was obvious that the distress was exceptionally real. The parent and I had many phone calls. The parent felt that they were in a battle with the child at these times, trying to get them to school. This increased the emotional upset and made the child even more resistant to attending school.

> *Eventually, a trigger was identified: the outbursts happened at some point in the week after the child had a scheduled phone call with another family member.*
>
> *Due to the background information shared with me by the parent, we both felt that the child actually needed the physical reassurance of being with this parent, following these phone calls. We both felt that to pressurise the child into attending would cause further trauma and that what the child actually needed was the love and reassurance of this parent at these times.*
>
> *We agreed that, if possible, the parent would bring the child for part of the day, but if the child was too distressed and they felt this would put too much pressure on the child, I would understand. The parent was absolutely brilliant at providing the care the child needed whilst also explaining that they would need to attend school and ensured that what was agreed was stuck to. The school arranged additional emotional support for the child. This arrangement lasted for many months before the child's outbursts and school refusal stopped altogether.*

My analysis of the two examples

Whilst writing these cases, I was struck with the similar needs of each child to be close to a loving parent. The school refusal could be seen as purely a school issue, but, in both cases, it appeared to me that separation anxiety and fear were at the root.

Anecdote 1

In the first case study, due to the chaotic and unexpected nature of the move, I felt that it was very important to provide a stable, consistent base. I was also aware that the parent's life had been turned upside down, as well as the child's. School attendance was important not only for the child but for the parent too so that they could have some much-needed respite. As the child was in a completely new setting both domestically and educationally, there was a great deal of boundary testing. It highlighted to me two key points that I wanted conveyed to the child through my actions:

- ◆ The first was that the child felt contained. I wanted the child to know that we could bear and deal with the emotion – that they were now safe and would be cared for.

◆ The second was that despite what had happened, the expectation of school or rather 'learning' still stood (i.e. they were not now going to call the shots). I felt strongly that this little person needed to be a child again and that the need for control came out of an understandable feeling of insecurity. In order to relinquish control and be a child, they needed to know we were trustworthy and dependable. The phrase we use at school for this is 'nurture within structure'.

Anecdote 2

The second case for me was about a child really needing to experience love and security from the family. The situation brought up such extreme anxieties, but due to my knowledge of the child's past, I knew these to be very real. I felt a forced separation would cause further trauma. I wasn't worried about creating an unhealthy dependency, as the child genuinely needed to know their existing parent was not going to disappear. I was also fortunate to know that the parent would not take advantage of this situation. The mental ills were as real as any physical ones.

Reflecting on my own emotions

Whilst writing about these, it brings to mind the feelings that I experience when I am called to a child who is visibly acting out their distress. I find that a few thoughts race through my mind. *Usually, I notice an increase in my heart rate.* In order to manage this, I tell myself to slow down so that my walking and speech do not convey panic to others. *I have to pay attention to my own breathing.*

In the first case, this definitely happened. *My mind was suddenly 'switched on' and running through it were many questions*: What on earth am I going to do? I cannot drag a child from a car so what do I do? If I don't manage this, will I be seen as a failure? Is this right for the child? *My heart bumped a little harder than normal in my chest.*

I was concerned as I was a complete stranger to the child. I really wanted them to feel that I was reliable and trustworthy so that they would feel safe. I always feel the weight of responsibility in these situations. I felt it very keenly in this case as the parent was looking to me and I really didn't know if I could sort this out, whether this would become an awful stalemate, or become worse in some, as yet, unknown way. *I remember thinking that I hope I have the inner resources to deal with the situation and that I'm making the right calls. It was not a comfortable place to be.*

When the child was left with me, screaming and shouting, I was really keen to keep things from escalating. I was concerned that the other staff member with me would pick up and follow my cues. *I try to use a calm, quiet voice and it really helps if the person with me does the same. I remember signalling to the other adult not to argue with the child and being so grateful when they understood.*

For me these times often have the *feel of a dance about them with the child saying or doing something and me replying with a small move or word.*

When I looked at the story book, my intention was that the *minimal conversation would help to stop the tension building* and take the pressure off the child, a way of being alongside without it demanding anything of them. I just hoped my approach was achieving this. When I saw the tiniest glimmer of interest, I turned the book a millimetre towards the child. All the time I was doing this, I felt hyper alert to the atmosphere in the room and any small changes: *I was completely fixed on 'reading' the child.* I hoped my responses were hitting the mark. This 'dance' went on for a long while. *It's hard to sit with so many unknowns, but I did have faith that it would work.*

Footnote from Dr Evans

This 'dance' that happens not just between educator and child but between mother and infant was first noticed and named the 'mother-infant dance' by Dan Stern (1977). He was at the fore of the research into studying the impact on development of the earliest non-verbal mother-infant communications (i.e. eye gazing, smiling and closely attuned interactions). Infants without these important early interactions were seen to have their development adversely impacted. We see in the anecdote described above how children who are struggling with their personal lives need the adults around them to be closely attuned. This visibly calms them and helps them to feel safe, ultimately reducing anxiety and enabling learning to happen.

7

Self-harming and depression

> **Health warning!**
>
> Self-harming and depression are separate but linked subjects and will thus be explored in this chapter individually, noting the links between them. They form part of the more extreme emotions and behaviours that educators are now having to face. This chapter inevitably has content that could be distressing but as educators we need to be able to face these so we can help. It is not helpful for us to feel powerless like the children who are struggling.
>
> If any of the issues trigger personal experiences, talk to a friend or colleague. You are part of a team in your school who have the capacity to support each other. If you feel, for personal reasons, wary of dealing with self-harm or depression, ask for help. This trust in colleagues and ability to know we're only human is an integral part of working in a containing and compassionate school culture.

Self-harm

Alarm bells

Self-harming for primary-age children historically rings alarm bells. As little as ten years ago, it was very infrequent in primary schools and was mostly the domain of secondary schools. However, research is now showing that

DOI: 10.4324/9781003454434-10

sadly it is on the increase. In 2021, BBC Radio 4's File on 4 programme discussed the fact that the number of children aged 9–12 admitted to hospital having intentionally hurt themselves rose from 221 in 2013–2014 to 508 in 2019–2020. This is an alarming doubling of self-harm.

Why has it doubled?

There are many reasons why such an alarming doubling of figures might take place. Some have been discussed in this book. Children nowadays are much more aware than previously of scary facts in our world, many of which, like wars, might make them feel powerless. They also have more pressure at a younger age from social media sites, which can be difficult for young children to negotiate and are platforms for bullying and excluding. Anxiety, depression and mood disorders are all factors that can lead to self-harm. We know that children are struggling more with these extreme emotions than previously.

What is self-harm?

Most young people who self-harm do it by cutting their skin with razor blades or whatever sharp object they can find. There are other self-harming acts such as severe scratching; banging and hitting one's body, especially the head; and carving and scraping into the skin. Self-harming often puts fear into the hearts of adults. It is an abhorrent thought and a very provoking act. Adults can feel repulsed, dismayed and afraid when children inflict wounds on their young, growing bodies.

Self-harm is classified in the *Diagnostic and Statistical Manual of Mental Health Disorders* (DSM)(2022) as Non-Suicidal Self-Injury Disorder (NSSI). It is defined as the deliberate, self-inflicted destruction of body tissue **without** suicidal intent. The authors point to the fact that non-suicidal and suicidal self-injury should be differentiated, although between the two there are many overlaps. This can be seen in clinical practice, where some children who are self-harming without suicidal intent can cut too deeply and put their lives at risk. It is important to know that 20% of children and young people were found in DSM studies to have suicidal intent when self-harming, **but,** although self-harm should be taken seriously, it is not always a sign of suicidal tendencies. The DSM also states that more girls than boys self-harm.

All schools have policies in place on how to react if they see a child has self-harmed. These policies create safety around a difficult and frightening subject. They can mitigate against the fear and distress, especially when working with children who are 11 years and below.

Why do children self-harm?

Self-harm is a sign of distress. It can be a way of expressing helplessness, powerlessness, anger and other difficult emotions. It can offer emotional release, where talking is too difficult. Some children do it as a way of self-punishment due to very low feelings of self-esteem. If we cause physical pain in our bodies, that pain temporarily takes away the mental and emotional pain. Neither emotional nor physical pain is experienced. Instead, there is a 'cutting off' from all thoughts or feelings. Although this is an effective relief, it is only a temporary fix, so children need to repeat the act when their overwhelming mental and emotional pain returns. Thus, the cycle of continual self-harm that we often see continues, where multiple signs are visible on the body.

What are the main factors that can cause self-harming behaviour?

The DSM found that the main factors that cause self-harm in children and adolescents are depression, anxiety and mood disorders. Less common are post-traumatic stress disorders (PTSD). High levels of emotional dysregulation and low qualities of life are also contributory factors.

What can we do about it?

It is essential that you share with a senior member of staff any signs of self-harm that you come across or suspect. Ensure you familiarise yourself with and follow school policies. Beyond this, there are lots of things you can do to help. It is really important that you don't feel as powerless as the child. You are the adult, with insight, empathy and understanding. You can definitely help.

Looking at the hidden thoughts and feelings

Try to see beyond the behaviour to the thoughts and feelings underneath. We have all entered that state of wanting to 'cut off' from painful thoughts or feelings. Cutting is a more extreme behaviour, but drinking a lot of alcohol, taking recreational drugs, overeating and undereating are behaviours we might use to numb aspects of pain. If, as adults, we can let our young people know that we are thinking about hidden thoughts and feelings behind their behaviour, they can feel immediately heard.

Don't be afraid to talk about it

If you suspect a child is self-harming, you can try to talk to them about it. You can let them know that you understand feelings that are overwhelming and seem too terrible to share. You can name feelings like anger and shame, and normalise them – we all have difficult feelings at times. You can even 'own up' that when you feel a bit sad, you might eat too much chocolate, for instance. This can help young people to open up, especially if they are just beginning down the self-harming path. **A word of warning** – if they refuse to discuss it, don't push the subject. You can, however, discuss with colleagues how you might introduce the subject into the curriculum (see Chapter 13 *Curriculum Opportunities to Discuss Emotive Themes* and Chapter 15 *The Power of the Arts: Using Powerful Emotive Texts to Integrate Learning Intentions*). As stated in the first paragraph of Chapter 13:

> *Instead of expecting children to discuss their own personal experiences of feelings such as loss, anger, worry and regret, curriculum links provide perfect opportunities to talk about these emotions at a safe distance from children's own lives.*

Be available

If children feel that they are in the adult's mind, that they are thought about and that he or she is interested in them, they will feel more noticed. This is the relational aspect of educating that is a vital part of bringing about trust between educators and students. Within this relationship of an adult being available for a child, safety is promoted and anxiety is reduced. Not only does this aid learning but also it creates an environment where children can feel safe enough to speak to adults.

It doesn't always last

Most children do not continue to self-harm into their late adolescent and adult years. Some need professional help but most do not.

The following table provides a useful tool for dealing with self-harm:

What you might see	What to do
Cuts or severe scratching on arms, legs or stomach	All educators have to be observant of children, especially during games lessons. If cuts or severe scratching are noticed, an allocated adult has to speak with the child, listen to them and discuss with them the need to tell their parents/carers. Inform parents/carers.

What you might see	What to do
Signs of anxiety, depression or unstable moods, which could lead to self-harm	All educators have to familiarise themselves with the tables of symptoms of anxiety or depression in this book (pages 68 and 83). Be aware of looking out for self-harm in children who appear to have some symptoms of anxiety or depression or who struggle to regulate their moods.
Children who self-harm and seek adult attention	Where possible, adults have to encourage children to talk about their worries, to put them in a worry box and to talk to someone they trust. Naming negative emotions reduces anxiety.
Children who self-harm and avoid adult attention	Educators have to ensure they encourage the whole class to share their worries. Normalise emotions around self-harm and, where possible, integrate them into the curriculum.

Kate's experiences of children self-harming

The invisible child (avoidant attachment style)

Self-harm can at times be very difficult to spot. I remember a child who had gone to great lengths to hide the cutting she was doing to her body. She was a very quiet child, exceptionally quiet since she began school, so it was even more difficult to identify the gradual change and desperation that had led her to her actions. If we are honest, we have all had that moment of making a mental list of our pupils and being unable to remember a child. We can go over and over the class list in our head, but still that child may not spring to mind.

In schools we are all clear about who our pupil premium children are, our children with English as an additional language (EAL), etc., as they are key focus groups nationally. Alongside these we also create lists of our 'vulnerable groups'. In common with many of you, I'm sure, we list our 'quiet undemanding pupils' and any pupil who is giving us a 'gut' feeling that something's not quite right. When we have pupil progress meetings, we then spend time considering these pupils, to make sure they are not slipping through the net, both academically and emotionally. It is a protective factor; we spend time attending to the particular needs of these quiet children, ensuring that they do not become 'invisible' just by virtue of not causing us any bother. Whilst this in itself would not stop a child self-harming (and we are not saying that any quiet child would self-harm), it does mean we're on the alert for changes and concerns.

The angry child (disorganised, controlling, traumatised attachment style)

As Angela has explained, not all self-harming is invisible. It can be especially distressing to watch a child who is so angry and has such low self-worth that they begin to hit themselves hard. I have experienced this, and it always makes me very sad. As Angela has described, it is important not to induce shame, so choosing our words carefully is helpful. If we react with horror, this potentially feeds into the child's own belief about themselves being in some way unlovable or lacking. In this situation, we use the phrase 'our bodies are not for hurting' (it can also be used when someone has hurt someone else too, with a small tweak to 'other people's bodies are not for hurting'). At first, it feels a little clumsy, but the beauty of the phrase is that it can be delivered calmly and with concern. It does not imply blame or shame. It is purely factual. Having a phrase ready also buys the adult some thinking time and supports them in remaining calm. When the incident is over, and the child is ready to talk, this phrase can be a helpful starting point, as it gives a little distance. The adult can talk about how distressed they were to see this as 'our bodies are not for hurting' and then 'wonder' about the events that led to this. This hopefully lessens the pressure on the child and allows them some control over the information they share.

The anxious child (resistant, ambivalent, anxious attachment style)

I worked with a child who appeared to be quite confident, in fact, at times, overconfident, rushing around organising peers, always 'busy' in the classroom. When this child was asked to stop, however, stand still or engage in conversation with an adult, they would pick very hard at the quicks around their fingers – so hard in fact that the skin was raw and ragged. Whilst this may not spring to mind as 'typical' self-harm, it was a way for the child to be distracted from a growing sense of anxiety and discomfort. Just like the invisible child, this child's anxiety could easily be missed.

As we have already acknowledged, teachers are not therapists. For some children, external professional support may be required. Whilst we are not able or expected to 'fix' pupils, we can take steps to provide an environment that feels safe and secure. We can acknowledge children's feelings and offer alternative ways of expressing emotion that release children from an overwhelming desire to hurt themselves.

Depression

What is depression?

The DSM definition of depression in children and adolescents is a depressed mood for most of the day, for more days than not, **for at least a year.** The

Depression Symptoms

- Feeling cut off
- Tired

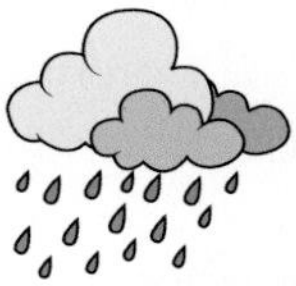

- Loss of appetite or comfort eating
- Feeling hopeless
- Low self-esteem
- Feeling guilty
- Irritability
- Lacking interest in anything
- Feeling tearful
- Feeling anxious
- Suicidal thoughts
- Self-harm
- Bullying
- Difficulty sleeping
- Poor concentration

Figure 7.1 Depression symptoms

depressed mood is not caused by medication. Main features of a depressed mood are as follows:

- ◆ Poor appetite or overeating
- ◆ Difficulty sleeping
- ◆ Tiredness
- ◆ Poor concentration
- ◆ Feelings of hopelessness

Fig. 7.1 shows additional features that can be helpful when considering whether a child in your class/school may have depression. **If symptoms haven't been apparent for a year, they are still worth noticing,** as the build up to the year is a pre-diagnosis state of mind, which can more easily be nipped in the bud to allay a diagnosis of depression.

Why do children get depressed?

Much of childhood depression is due to family relationships, as children and adolescents are still very dependent on parents and are unable to escape situations like domestic violence, extreme poverty, mental or physical illness in adults or siblings, illness or death of a family member and alienation from one's country, all of which can contribute to making a child feel depressed.

Another main factor in childhood depression is children feeling different in their peer groups. They may be outstandingly academic to the point where other children see them as odd. They might struggle academically or with sports. Children are very good at spotting who is not 'normal' and, unless they are helped to celebrate differences in brain functions, known as neuro-divergence, they will easily isolate children who stand out from the crowd. A school culture that can embrace children's different skills, abilities and tendencies is likely to make all children more accepting and tolerant of their peers.

What does depression look like in a child in school?

Depression is different in flavour to anxiety; it speaks of hopelessness and powerlessness. A depressed child in school may be the one who sits with their head in their hands or on the desk, who yawns, who seems bored and who only joins in activities from the side lines. They may also be oversensitive, tearful and irritable, making peer relationships difficult and painful. This can make them subject to bullying or being bullied. You may notice weight gain or loss, which may exacerbate the bullying/bullied cycle and affect self-esteem. They may not trust adults. They are often the children who won't speak out about their emotions or about self-harming behaviour.

What can we do about it?

As with self-harming, it is essential that you share with a senior member of staff any signs of depression that you come across or suspect. Ensure you familiarise yourself with and follow school policies. You can decide with your colleagues to keep an eye on what appear to be early stages of depression, to 'watch and wait' whilst simultaneously doing all you can to engage the child and the parents/carers. It can be really helpful to meet with the parents/carers, to explore with them how their child is at home and to gain their trust so they might share family issues. Regular meetings like this can contain the adults, who are then more able to contain their children.

How to help in the classroom

Bored, listless children can be irritating to educators as they can easily spread their negativity amongst the class. They are actually desperately projecting their unbearable emotions onto others. The message to you, the adult, is, *'Please help me. I feel so rubbish but I just can't ask for help. If I show any vulnerability, I might cry in front of the whole class'*. If as adults we can let our young people know that we are thinking about what's behind their behaviour, they can feel immediately heard.

Bring difficult emotions, including feelings of depression, into the curriculum (see reference above to Chapters 13 and 15). It can feel overwhelming for a child to feel tired and tearful. We all know that feeling. Normalise it. Relate it to commonly shared physical illnesses like a bad cold. Children can share in class discussions how they feel when ill – tired, tearful and frustrated. Discuss feeling ill in your body or your mind. The key is normalising, normalising more and then normalising again! It is only by bringing mental and emotional illness into the open that the stigma and feelings of shame can be reduced.

If you notice a child is depressed, you can try to talk to them about it, but first you need to ensure you have a trusting relationship with them. Where possible, try to engage the depressed child in jobs around the classroom that might involve quiet moments of time with you. This replicates an early parent-infant relationship where the child might be sitting at a table drawing while the parent prepares a meal. The parent is alongside the child, not intrusively but availably, creating a feeling of safety and familiarity, which is a powerful non-verbal part of building trust.

Kate's experiences of children with depression

In schools we often have a window into different family worlds. We may be aware of circumstances or history that in any other job would remain private and unknown. This privileged information can help us to empathise with and support children who find school challenging. I remember a child during my early career, whose life was particularly difficult and emotionally sparse. This child had chosen to retreat and appeared to view the world without hope. All tasks were met with the same low, emotionless approach, without a glimmer of joy. This included structured time in the classroom and unstructured time at play. It was almost as if the child felt they did not deserve their place in the world.

Conversations were difficult as the child would nod, shake a head or reply with the least number of words possible. Interestingly, the child was never rude or impolite, rather you really felt the child's discomfort at having been noticed and spoken with. People's usual reaction was to close the conversation down, as quickly as possible, as continuing seemed to cause pain for the child. This unfortunately confirmed to the child that they had nothing to offer.

The school looked to provide adult support in the classroom. Following no positive change, this then moved to a small group for academic and social/ emotional work, then bespoke one to one provision. This had no effect. Advisory teachers had been called, assessments undertaken, all advice was followed but still nothing appeared to shift for this child. Not only did the child feel hopeless but staff were beginning to feel like this too.

School staff looked carefully at the symptoms and possible causes of this behaviour and a decision was made to employ a play therapist to work with the child. The form of therapy did not require the child to speak unless they wanted to. The sessions took place weekly for a period of three months. During this time, it was like watching the slow blossoming of a flower. In very small ways, the child began to show emotion, to allow a small smile or to respond to a greeting. Friendships started to form. The change was remarkable.

It doesn't always last

As with self-harm, most children do not continue to experience depression into their late adolescent and adult years. Some need professional help but many do not. They can go on to form their own lives as adults, with more of a sense of agency and hopefulness as they gain more independence and life experience.

As teachers, we can offer a high-quality education to support all learners and we can provide bespoke support within a caring, compassionate environment which aids the reduction of anxiety and therefore frees the child's mind to focus on learning. We are not expected to take the place of therapists, but we can utilise all the tools at our disposal to develop the independence, the tenacity and the self-belief of pupils. The following chapters are full of rich examples to help you do just that.

PART III

Supporting the learning to reduce anxiety

8

Pupil self-efficacy

Shirley now outlines the different features of classroom learning which have a direct impact on children's anxiety levels. Beginning with the foundation of children's self-efficacy, and how we can radically improve it, she then discusses the following key elements of organisation: learning support partners, learning frameworks of learning intentions and success criteria, easing the cognitive load and the reassuring impact of live, in-lesson feedback.

What is self-efficacy? How does it link with anxiety?

Self-efficacy is ***your belief in your ability to achieve***: a critical component of being a successful and anxiety-free learner. Unfortunately, many of the structures and systems in place in our schools, as well as behaviours, actually lower children's self-efficacy. Children naturally compare themselves to their peers: their appearance, clothes, likes, dislikes and so on. In school, children's main point of comparison is their perception of who is 'the cleverest' and where they fit in the hierarchy. This leads to fear of making mistakes or not understanding. Being in the bottom group or being slower than everyone else must mean that they are stupid, 'thick' or inadequate. If schools make explicit their expectations of children based on their perceptions of their ability, this becomes a self-fulfilling prophecy, often leading to high anxiety and projection of negative emotions.

DOI: 10.4324/9781003454434-12

Now apply the above to teachers and think about whether there are systems or more subtle ways in which teachers are compared to other teachers, thus lowering their self-efficacy. If we want children to have 'marvellous mistakes', then teachers should be just as excited by them! Kate Moss tackles the issues involved in creating high self-efficacy for teachers in Chapter 17, *The Role of the School Leader.*

Pupil self-efficacy

Comparing yourself to others

Even higher achievers can feel embarrassed by clear comparisons with other children and end up hiding their ability for fear of ridicule of being 'brainy'. Although higher achievers generally do well in any context, the impact of explicit comparison systems, such as grading, comparative rewards (stickers, stars and housepoints), ego-related praise and ability grouping, is to demoralise lower achievers to the extent that, over time, they avoid investing effort in subjects or lessons which would lead to more failure (Black and Wiliam, 1998). While they have no choice but to be present in such a culture, children's anxiety can only be exacerbated. All is not lost, however, as many schools now have eliminated explicit comparative systems and report that children are less anxious without them and achieve more successfully.

The barriers to self-efficacy, all a result of comparisons, are as follows and are now explained in full:

a) **Teachers/support staff talking or behaving to children 'differently' depending on their perceived 'ability': how we engage with each child.**
b) **Fear of error or not understanding.**
c) **Comparative rewards.**
d) **Ego-related praise.**
e) **Ability grouping and labelling.**
f) **Negative peer relationships.**

How we engage with each child

If we can have high expectations for every student (Rubie-Davies, 2017), it will lead to progress for all, but there are physical factors involved (as well as organisational factors) in convincing students that you have equal expectations regardless of their level of achievement.

We tend to give more *excitable praise* to lower achievers but more *critical comment* to higher achievers (Meyer, 1992). This is a give-away to children that you think of them differently and have different expectations of them. Interviewed lower achievers in Meyer's study, when asked why the teacher was so pleased with their work, replied *she didn't think I'd be able to do it*. Thus, our *actions and words* convey our expectations based on our perceptions of their ability, leading to a self-fulfilling prophecy. Our body language also sends powerful messages to children about how we are judging them.

Strategies
1 Use the same tone of voice and choice of language for every child, without being over excited, when commenting on their achievement.   2 Make sure your body language doesn't send messages that you have any negative expectations or feelings towards individuals. You might believe that you convey that you have their best interests at heart, but a shrug, a raised eyebrow, an impatient tone of voice, a tapping foot, a sigh, conveys in very real terms to children how we really feel!

Children need to be convinced that you believe in them and that they can achieve so that they feel not only safe but also worthy. *High self-efficacy leads to a feeling of pride rather than anxiety.*

Acting out, projection, panic attacks and so on are often the consequence of feeling inadequate and unseen as important in the teacher's eyes, even though we might believe we treat all children equally.

Fear of getting it wrong

Errors invite opportunity. They should not be seen as embarrassments, signs of failure or something to be avoided. They are exciting, because they indicate a tension between what we now know and what we could know: they are signs of opportunities to learn and they are to be embraced.

Hattie (2012)

Fear of failure is something children often experience, especially if there are consequences of their mistakes which make them feel demoralised, negatively judged or deemed to be 'thick'. Young children want their teacher's approval, and all children are fearful of being ridiculed or put down by higher achievers or unkind children in their class. Building a culture where there is equity in the classroom, through mixed ability and no comparative rewards, as well as activating children as learning resources for one another (see Chapter 9), goes a long way towards achieving a mutually respectful, kind environment. It is the teacher's words and sentiments, however, which have the most power. Instead of sympathising over mistakes, express excitement that they are on the brink of learning something new; instead of praising finishing quickly, praise those concentrating well or challenging themselves. Children need to be told not only the importance of making mistakes in helping us grow our intelligence (*when we are thinking hard more neural connections are made*) but also the difference between 'slips', which are usually able to be self-corrected once pointed out, and misconceptions, or not understanding what to do, which needs input either from a teacher, support adult or another child. Dweck (2016) suggested that effort is not enough to be successful: it is a combination of practice, effort, time and input which leads to success.

Strategies
1 Make a PETI (practise, effort, time, input) poster and ask children to use this language when they get stuck, to describe what they think they need. It is much more empowering to say 'I need input' than 'I need help'. 2 Make a 'stuck' poster to give children strategies before they seek input.

| **What do you need?**

Practise

Effort

Time

Input | **Are you stuck?**

1 Don't panic! Count slowly to 10.
2 Read the question again.
3 Are there any resources which might help?
4 Do you need more input?
   -ask a student who knows
   -ask an adult |

Comparative reward systems

The damaging element with reward systems is the comparison effect, not the reward itself: if, for one activity/piece of work/learning experience, only some children get the sticker, star or house point while others do not, the effect is to make complacent those who get them and to demoralise and make anxious those who don't. The problem is the 'invisibility effect': we don't see how this affects each child's self-efficacy, as they don't ever question our judgement. Instead they take the giving of rewards as an explicit message about their worth as a learner and often for that subject. It doesn't make any difference which criteria are used in giving rewards: it is the comparison that matters.

It is interesting that in South East Asia rewards in schools don't exist because their culture sees education and learning as the reward itself (Stigler and Hiebert, 1999). I believe we have become complacent in the west about the incredible gift of education, thinking that it is not enough and needs some kind of token.

> **The effect of giving rewards to some children and not others for the same activity is to make complacent those who get them and to demoralise and make anxious those who don't.**

Comparative rewards have proven short-term impact only, and for behaviour, don't actually work. Reward systems lead to children avoiding challenging tasks, making excuses for poor performance and lowering their belief in their ability to achieve (Black and Wiliam, 1998). They also stop children becoming self-regulating through intrinsic motivation.

Rewards that don't compare

Anything that all children know they will get over time is clearly altogether different and a good way to celebrate individual successes and progress. Every child, for instance, can be 'child of the week' in a Friday assembly, as long as they are told at the beginning of the year that they will all be included; every child can appear in the 'Golden Book' as long as they know they will all be in it; every child in an infant class can be given a sticker at the end of the day for whole class achievement.

> **Clarke's feedback from many learning teams has a running theme: children don't notice when the rewards are removed, are less anxious without them and focus entirely on their learning rather than on gaining a reward.**

Praise

> Ego-related praise can undermine resilience, as it sends messages that it is the student rather than his or her persistence in learning that determines success.

Hattie and Clarke (2019)

Of course we should praise children, but how we do it is significant in its effect. Ego-related praise (*You're so good at this, Clever girl!, I knew you'd be able to do this quickly as you're so good at maths*) has a worse impact on student learning than not giving it at all (Kluger and DeNisi, 1996). Task, or achievement – related praise or feedback, and learning behaviour – related praise leads to children being more engaged in and less anxious about their learning: for example **I like your alliteration here … and I noticed you managing distractions and really concentrating.** This approach especially helps to reduce anxiety in avoidantly attached children, who cannot manage the directness of ego-related praise. For the reasons given, however, we should avoid ego-related praise with **all** children, if we want a learning orientation rather than a performance orientation.

Verbally praising children throughout the day in this way, via on-the-move feedback and in all teacher commentary, makes it clear that it is their learning and achievement we value, not the receiving of a tokenistic reward. Achievement, progress and using 'learning powers' of concentrating, not giving up, co-operating and so on are reward enough and become a source of great pride for all children.

Ability grouping

Five hundred studies from 14 meta-analyses on ability grouping, analysed by John Hattie (2009), resulted in an effect size of 0.12 (where 0.4 is one year's progress for one year of doing it): a very low impact on student achievement, with outcomes of very little change in attainment but profound effects on student self-efficacy.

> *Where there is low self-efficacy, in this case caused by ability grouping, there is anxiety about learning and being in school.*

South East Asian countries do not group by ability and see mixed ability as a gift: the opportunity for different strategies and learning from one another. With frequently changing learning partners (see Chapter 9), children do indeed learn from one another and develop a sense of equal opportunities and mutual respect. Without ability labels, they feel confident to challenge themselves – another example of a self-fulfilling prophecy: with high expectations for all, we get high levels of progress.

Self-fulfilling prophecies: The Pygmalion effect and the Attachment Needs Cycle

The Pygmalion effect: teachers' expectations Pymalion was a Greek sculptor who fell in love with a statue he had carved of a beautiful woman. He kissed and doted on the statue, which then turned into a woman, and his expectations were realised. Similarly, Rosenthal and Jacobson (1968) told teachers that half of their students were 'late bloomers' and would 'bloom' during the year, and half would not, based on tests that they had administered. This was all fictitious, as the 'late bloomers' were chosen randomly. As the researchers suspected, at the end of the year more 'bloomers' outperformed 'non-bloomers'. Given that the assignment was random, the difference claimed was a direct result of the higher expectations of the teachers for those students. Observations revealed that teachers spoke to the so called late bloomers differently to other children and would drill down asking further questions until the right answer was reached if one of those children gave a wrong answer in class. It seems the 'late bloomers' were made to feel special and encountered continuous success when questioned. The graphic produced by Rosenthal and Jacobson to explain the effect of teachers' beliefs about children's ability can be seen in Fig. 8.1.

Links with the Attachment Needs Cycle This self-fulfilling prophecy is reproduced and mirrored here in Figs. 8.2 and 8.3. When a child is securely attached, things only get better for them. When the attachment is insecure, however, it goes from bad to worse, as the cycle continues.

Negative peer relationships

Graham Nuthall, in his book 'The Hidden Lives of Learners' (2007), after analysing transcripts of hundreds of conversations between children in classrooms while they were working and unheard by any adults, identified three worlds that children live in:

- ◆ The public world, governed by the teacher
- ◆ The semi-private world governed by children's peer relationships
- ◆ The private world: the mind of the child.

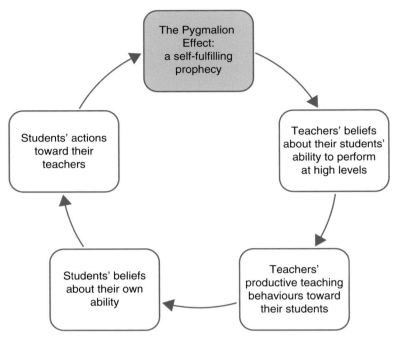

Figure 8.1 The Pygmalion effect

It is the semi-private world which is most threatening for children because it describes their peer relationships unsupervised by adults. Bullying and cliques can be found in this world, with the perpetrators very skilled at making sure they are not seen or heard by any adult. Getting

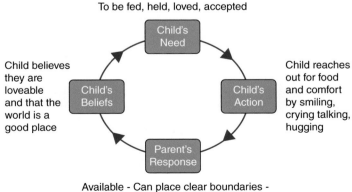

Figure 8.2 Secure attachment cycle

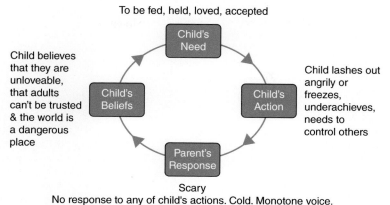

Attachment Needs Cycle - Traumatised

Figure 8.3 Traumatised attachment cycle

to the bottom of bullying or unkind behaviour is notoriously difficult in schools (see Chapter 2 for the psychology and advice about bullying) because children generally deny all wrongdoing and might even blame the victim. A child might have a wonderful relationship with the teacher but be extremely anxious about being in school because of these often invisible factors.

Nuthall states as follows:

Classes in which academic achievement was the only criterion for success in the teacher's eyes, tended to develop a fixed hierarchical status system in which the academically successful were always on top and constantly putting down those who were less successful.

He concludes that we need to convey our appreciation of all children's skills and traits rather than prioritising only academic achievement.

This links with the ongoing commentary I described as effective 'praise', in which we constantly name children's achievement and learning behaviour. If we add to this acts of kindness and respect, for example, we are conveying values which will soon become theirs.

The use of random learning partners changing weekly in primary classrooms is another way to cut through cliques that often help nurture bullying because children are constantly changing who they sit with, work with, learn with and developing new friendships with.

9

Effective learning partners

Scary classrooms

Many people's childhood memories will be of being pounced on by the teacher to answer a question when they had no idea what to say. Being in the 'hot seat' in front of your peers is scary for all of us. Many high-achieving teenagers deliberately opt out of answering questions to which they know the answer, out of fear of being deemed too 'brainy,' and many low-achieving children often freeze even if they know the answer, out of fear of failure and extreme self-consciousness. *Student-to-teacher feedback* was found by Hattie (2012) to be more important than teacher-to-student feedback: that constant quest to find out what is in their heads, to find out how much they understand or know at this moment. Teachers know that this matters, so extensive whole-class questioning is common practice to gather this all-important feedback from students to teacher, but how is it best to organise children to help them feel supported and contained, rather than vulnerably exposed?

Think, pair, share

We have come a long way since the days of teachers giving no 'wait time' (Rowe, 1974) and asking for hands up, thus excluding most of the class from doing the thinking or the answering. Thankfully for children's self-efficacy and therefore their feeling of being safe in the classroom to speak

DOI: 10.4324/9781003454434-13

in front of others, it is now common practice for children to be asked to discuss the teacher's question with a partner first, before responses are taken. This has extended their wait time and thinking time and enabled children to learn from each other, boosting their confidence. This became known as 'think, pair, share' and transformed questioning in the classroom.

Random learning partners, changing weekly works best

Clarke's work over 22 years (Clarke, 2014, 2021a) found that the greatest impact for learning partners to be able to effectively learn from one another, as well as to increase their self-efficacy and lower any anxiety over speaking in front of others, was to be **paired randomly and to change weekly**.

Children need to experience a range of both cognitive and social partnerships in the classroom in order to learn from others, teach others, reassure, be patient, respect all personalities and learn to work with anyone, so random pairings was found to be most successful. Being in mixed ability also reduces anxiety, and changing partners weekly means they don't get a chance to be 'cast in role' as the helper, 'helpee' or any other position of influence. These partnerships are not just devices for answering questions; they are also their learning partners for the week to be a support during lessons and during independent work, reducing possible anxiety. Children love having a partner to discuss their learning with, instead of feeling that they are alone in the classroom with everyone in the room possibly judging them if they don't understand or give the wrong answer.

Strategies
The organisational devices which work best are as follows: • Random choosing via named lollysticks, a randomiser or laminated photos in a bag on Monday morning • Reception children have a 'magic spot' on the carpet for the week • Partners move their seats unless they are on the autism spectrum • Make 3s for children with English as an additional language or any language or severe behaviour issues

- Co-construct success criteria for 'being a good learning partner' and display in the room, used for self-evaluation and constant reference
- On Friday last thing, before shaking hands and thanking their partner, children write a positive statement in each other's 'compliment books' about why they enjoyed learning with them

The impact of random learning partners, reported by teachers

- ◆ It's inclusive, so children are more likely to confidently answer questions in front of the class
- ◆ Better behaviour
- ◆ Greater focus as no more hands up but picked to answer questions via named lollysticks (the pair can answer, not just the child whose name is randomly called)
- ◆ Higher quality work and writing
- ◆ Develop mutual respect and appreciation of each other's strengths and weaknesses
- ◆ Make new friends thus breaking up cliques
- ◆ Great support for those with no English and language issues
- ◆ Learning from each other

Anecdote

In my class the randomiser placed the highest achiever with the lowest achiever, who has speech and language problems. At first they were like deer in the headlights. The higher achiever's attitude changed for the better and he praised the lower achiever for her accomplishments. Simultaneously her language skills developed, having his higher level language to learn from.

Gemma Bain
Ysgol Llandrillo yn Rhos

Anecdote

Historically, one high-achieving child in my class wasn't able to work with a learning partner. She wasn't kind or helpful and is possibly on the spectrum, so had to sit by herself. Reassured by the high success rate of Clarke's random talk partners, I have included her and randomly paired her every week with everyone else. The difference in her attitude and ability to help her peers has been huge. She now feels more included and makes a helpful and successful partner.

Lucy Jones
Holy Trinity C of E Primary

Anecdote

One child receiving treatment which compromises his immune system so he can't come to school has a robot with a web cam, microphone and speaker, so he can be 'in class' (see Fig. 9.1). He controls the robot by an app on his iPad, and having random talk partners means he can have a partner like everyone else. He is not in school but still gets the full range of social experiences and the ability to learn with his classmates.

Gemma Hall
Dorchester Primary

Figure 9.1 AV1 robot by No Isolation (Credit: noisolation.com/av1)

10

Clear learning intentions and co-constructed success criteria

How will I know what the teacher expects from me?

For a child to know the purpose of a lesson (learning intentions) and what they have to do to achieve success (success criteria) seems an obvious requirement to maximise children's chances of achievement and progress, yet it is only relatively recently that they have become a routine part of the structure of a lesson. My own memory of being at school was that everything was activity focused. The teacher might have known what they were hoping we would learn, but we simply knew that we had to do the activity, whether that was a page from a text book, some work set from the board, a title given for an essay or a drawing of a shoe. You listened to instructions and guessed how you would be judged. Taking a lead from the highest achievers in the class was the best clue for getting the required comment or gold star, but often you just had to ask more questions of the teacher to try to ascertain exactly what she or he was looking for. My first report at my girls' grammar school stated 'Shirley asks too many

DOI: 10.4324/9781003454434-14

questions'! **My memory was of tangible anxiety that I was not sure of what was expected of me.** An example from my first year at the school:

Anecdote

On one occasion, at age 11, after reading through 'The Merchant of Venice' as a class, having only partial understanding of its plot, we were set the essay title 'The character of Bassanio.' I remember sitting at home reading and trying to understand the text and feeling a sense of dread and panic. Was I the only one who felt like this? The teacher was awe inspiring and I didn't want to disappoint her. I had no idea that her teaching was inadequate, simply that it must be me that was inadequate. I walked to the nearby library before it closed and asked a librarian if he could tell me anything about Bassanio. From his kind description I managed to write something and, to my relief, was graded A minus.

My anxiety at the time is illustrated by, over 50 years later, my ability to recall every detail, including the face of the kind librarian and even his tone of voice.

A key point here is that I truly believed that the fault was mine and not the teacher's.

Reimagined lesson: letting the children into the secret: frameworks, success criteria and knowing what good ones look like

Make clear what they are learning and lay the groundwork

Now imagine, instead, that teacher first making clear what was going on in the play, then introducing the learning intention for today and tomorrow, which was *To create an effective characterisation* with the context of Bassanio. We then talk about Bassanio with our talk partners, gathering observations about him that are written up at the front, with links to quotations.

Co-construct the success criteria while seeing what a good one looks like

She then shows us a characterisation of a different Shakespearian character from a previous class student and asks us, in pairs, to come up with one feature at a time which we can spot which makes it a characterisation. As she writes the features up, she also writes, in brackets, an example from the text so that we see exactly what each success criterion might look like. We end up with a number of criteria for a characterisation. *She explains that we don't necessarily have to use all of these —they are a toolkit of good suggestions.*

L.I. To create an effective characterisation

Success criteria:

- **Extrovert or introvert?**
- **Examples of their personality (with quotes)**
- **Attitude to others (quotes)**
- **Attitude to self: conceited/self-critical**
- **Appearance if it shows something about their character**

Comparing good with poor to clarify what good writing looks like

We are then given two examples of previously written characterisations of Shakespeare's characters: one which includes all of those possible success criteria and is well written and another which includes all of the features but is not well written, with no detail or interesting language. The two pieces are read aloud, and we then, in pairs, decide one thing that the good piece has which the poor piece doesn't and, as a class, start compiling the differences between the two. The teacher gets us to think about the impact on the reader: how the words used make us feel and the images they produce.

Ready to apply

Only then are we asked to go back to our class brainstorm of observations of Bassanio before being set the characterisation for homework. Now I feel empowered, full of knowledge and clear about how my work will be judged. *I am anxiety free.*

Starting from the planning stage

So the starting point is knowing the learning intention of the lesson. There might be two – knowledge (e.g. to know about the evacuation programme in World War II) and skill through which the knowledge is applied (e.g. to write a diary entry).

Teachers have much more support in coming up with learning intentions in the first place, if their country has introduced a National Curriculum. A school's planning now starts with the requirements of the National Curriculum, the frameworks of concepts to be taught and then the breakdown of those, usually by schools, into units of work, often broken down

Art Curriculum Overview

Team 2	**The Great Fire:** **Skills:** Painting (mixing colours) and collage **Inspiration:** Romanticism (Turner) Brit Pop (Nicholas Munro) **Outcome:** To produce a depiction of The Great Fire using paint and silhouette **Recap:** Mixing paints and collage (T1) Romanticism/Constable (T1)	**Inspiration:** Turner and Munro	**Outcome:**
	Heroes and Villains: **Skills:** Drawing and collage **Inspiration:** Pop Art (Peter Blake) **Outcome:** To produce a picture of heroes and villains inspired by Pop Art montages **Recap:** Drawing and collage (T1)	**Inspiration:** Peter Blake	**Outcome:**
	Towns and Cities: **Skills:** Printing/Etching **Inspiration:** Stephen Wiltshire **Outcome:** To produce print/etching of a cityscape/building	**Inspiration:** Stephen Wiltshire	**Outcome:**

Figure 10.1 Art curriculum framework for six- to seven-year-olds (Langford Primary School, Hammersmith and Fulham)

further into possible learning intentions. Langford School, Hammersmith and Fulham, created frameworks for each subject from key concepts to questions they want children to be able to answer by the end of each week. Fig. 10.1 shows their framework for art and how this breaks down for Year 2 (six- and seven-year-olds). By having an exciting, well-thought-out curriculum, with inspiring lessons, children are more likely to be distracted from their possible anxieties and able to 'get lost' in the learning and the tasks.

Co-constructing the success criteria

Success criteria are simply a breakdown of the skill learning intention, giving either steps or ingredients Clarke (2021b). Once children have these, they not only know what they have to do to achieve, they also have a means of self-evaluating, all of which gives children a sense of greater ownership over their learning and encourages them to become more confidently independent. Children find it much less daunting to seek more input for one of the success criteria, for instance, than simply telling a partner or a teacher that they are stuck or don't know what to do.

Co-constructing the success criteria gives children even more ownership over their learning, as they have been part of the creation of what they have to do. Most techniques involve presenting children with good examples

Mars Bar Cake	How to make delicious crunchy Mars Bar Cakes
Put the Mars bar in the big pan.	**Ingredients**
Cut up the Mars bar before you put it in the big pan.	• 2 medium sized Mars Bars • 50g Rice Krispies • 25g butter
Weigh out the butter. Put in pan with the Mars bar.	**You will need**
Turn on the heat.	• A large pan and a baking tray or dish
Wait till it gets all gooey.	• Knife and board
Add the Rice Krispies and stir like the wind.	• Mixing spoon • Scales
Put into a tray and put in the fridge.	1 Grease your dish or tray to stop your cake from sticking to the sides
Don't forget to grease the tray before you add the mixture otherwise it sticks really hard and you can't get it out.	2 Weigh out the butter 3 Using your knife carefully cut the butter and Mars Bars into small pieces and place them in a big pan.
Delicious!!	4 Etc., etc.

Figure 10.2 Poor and good examples of instructions

from which they spot the criteria being applied. My favourite method, and the most powerful, is presenting a good example alongside a poor example (all anonymous pieces from a previous class of course) and asking 'What has this person done that the other person hasn't?'

Fig. 10.2 is a perfect example of good and poor examples used to co-construct the success criteria for the learning intention 'To write instructions'. Notice that the resulting criteria are generic to any context and so can be transferred and used every time this skill is revisited by this class.

Co-constructed resulting success criteria

Learning Intention: To write instructions
Remember to

- List ingredients or items needed
- Include measurements
- Use bullet points, number or letters
- List the steps to take
- Start each step with an imperative verb
- Include diagrams or pictures if necessary

Strategies

Tips for co-constructing success criteria

1 Creating generic criteria for skills which are used often (e.g. instructions, newspaper article, poster, invitation, letter, persuasive writing, balanced argument and mathematical calculations) means they can be transferred to any context. Children start to internalise the ingredients which increases their self-confidence.

2 When explaining a new skill, model this silently while writing on the whiteboard so that children's working memories are not overwhelmed by trying to watch, follow and listen. When you have finished, ask them to talk to their partner about what you demonstrated: 'What did I just do? Tell your partner.' They will be more focused and relaxed.

3 With step-by-step criteria, ask 'What did we do first?', 'What did we do next?', etc. so that they are not overwhelmed with too much to think about.

4 With fiction writing analyse at least two good but different examples to stop children copying the style of one example and to have more examples of excellent words and phrases.

5 Focus on the impact on the reader with children's fiction writing and make clear that the success criteria are just a toolkit rather than compulsory elements such as those in a maths calculation.

Impact of clarifying what is being learnt and how to achieve it

The following quotes, from teachers from Clarke's action research learning teams, illustrate the impact of sharing learning intentions and co-constructing success criteria (for more, go to www.shirleyclarke-education. org). I have made bold those comments which show reducing anxiety through greater understanding, more clarity and greater success.

> Teachers had compared good with poor examples to generate the criteria. **Children know what good looks like, are more independent and more successful.**
>
> *Surrey Learning Team*

Children were asked to spot a mistake in maths, then told me what each step was. **Children talked in pairs about the steps to success, which really helped lower achievers**.

Taunton Learning Team

By modelling silently the steps for multiplying fraction, children were able to create the success criteria. **They had greater understanding and greater achievement**.

Taunton Learning Team

Success criteria enable children to identify errors at an early stage. **A less confident child in my class said 'Wow! I didn't think I could do such a good piece of work, and I got it finished!'**

Stockport Learning Team

In my school attainment levels went up from 87% to 92%. **Children are asking for help and extra work for success criteria that they feel they have not achieved. This is seen as a huge leap in confidence from the previous mindset of 'I'm no good at this'**.

Scotland Learning Team

A child on the Special Needs registry said '**Do they do success criteria in secondary schools, because I really know what I'm doing with them?**' In one Individual Education Plan box he had previously written 'Not annoying people around me' in answer to 'What helps you learn?' This time he had written '**Success criteria help me learn.**'

N. Wales Learning Team

11

Easing the cognitive load

How memory works

Our memory is made up of three parts: the sensory memory (everything we're seeing, hearing, etc.), the working memory (what we're focusing on in the moment) and the long-term memory. In order to remember anything, the information has to first travel from the working memory to the long-term memory. As Willingham (2009) famously said *Memory is the residue of thought*, so if we haven't thought about it or focused on it, we can't possibly remember it. So how long does a new piece of knowledge stay in our long-term memory? The answer is deceptively simple: the more we have retrieved that knowledge, the stronger the storage strength, so the longer we will remember it for. We used to think that testing children too much was bad for them, but it turns out that the more they are tested (so that they can repeatedly retrieve the knowledge), the longer they will remember it for! This explains why many of us can still recall our times tables after years of hardly using them: we retrieved them so many times in our education so that they are remembered forever.

Why is this important to know when considering reducing anxiety in the classroom?

Unfortunately, our working memory is flawed. We can only, without props, hold on to about seven individual items of information at any one time. We all encounter this when receiving a long reference number in our phones, which needs to be transferred to another place in our phones. We can't

DOI: 10.4324/9781003454434-15

remember the numbers (if there are more than seven or eight) unless we write them down or transfer in more than one step.

How am I going to remember all this?

Imagine going to hear a lecture during which the speaker has no slides and you have no handouts or pen and paper. How much do you think you would be able to recall of the talk? When I present to teachers, I make sure they all have copies of the slides, with space beside each one to write any notes, as well as summaries of the talk and pen and paper. I talk to the slides and also show video clips to further help teachers understand the content. I have often been to talks in which the speaker shows slides, but there are no copies for the delegates, so people are frantically trying to copy the information from slides they like rather than listening to the speaker. These days, teachers in that situation just tend to take a photograph of the slide, but that is another distraction taking the listener away from really thinking about what the speaker is saying.

I think I'll just switch off …

Now imagine a class of children listening to a teacher talk. They won't be able to remember it all unless there are ways to 'ease the cognitive load'. When they lose track of what is being said or described, children tend to use one of two strategies: they switch off and stop listening or start to talk to another pupil. Adults do the same if watching anything on a screen that doesn't hold their attention! Clearly easing the cognitive load is only one part of the picture: the lesson has to be broken down into parts and be accessible enough to be understood, as well as interesting enough to not be boring. The independent work set has to be achievable or supported enough that it is achievable.

Throughout this book, a common cause of children's anxiety is described as rooted in the learning environment. Enabling children to have support to process information and to sustain their attention and motivation during lessons is key to relieving anxiety caused by their learning. The classroom strategies described, as features of formative assessment, form a jigsaw of powerful elements to make learning as anxiety free as possible: through the high self-efficacy ethos (Chapter 8), supportive learning partners (Chapter 9), clear learning intentions, success criteria and knowing what good ones look like (Chapter 10) and enabling children to be able to hold on to the enormous amount of new learning they are faced with every day (this chapter).

The following strategies used by teachers in the classroom to support children's working memories will help children hold on to the knowledge being imparted, or a skill being described, so that they can relax in the knowledge that they don't have to remember everything right now, in the moment.

Strategies

- If using PowerPoint, print out one copy of the slides, enlarged, to display on the working wall for that subject so that they still exist and can be referenced.
- Create a final summary slide of the key points and give a copy to each child to be kept in a place where it won't get lost (e.g. a pocket in the back of the relevant exercise book).
- When children are able to take notes, provide 'rough books'.
- Stick permanent Perspex on every display board so that they can be used not only for putting up paper posters, etc. but also as an extension to the whiteboard.
- Give children a knowledge organiser for every topic. This should consist of key information you don't want them to forget, such as key events and key people or facts or rules related to core subjects. The knowledge organiser needs to be accessible and specifically referred to so that children have to think about the content. These are usually used as the basis for quick quizzes, to aid retrieval practice. Fig. 11.1 is a good example of an accessible knowledge organiser from Reach Academy in Feltham, London.

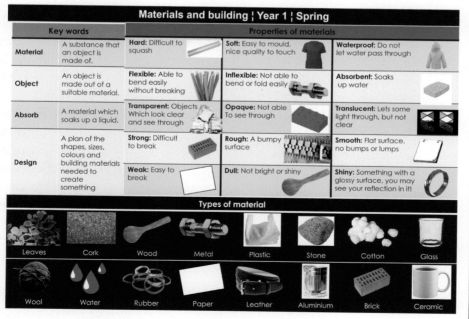

Figure 11.1 Knowledge organiser for five- and six-year-olds (Reach Academy, Feltham)

- When describing a new skill, model the process silently. Apparently talking as you're writing on the smart board overwhelms children's working memories, so tell them you're switching your voice off and just to watch. Teachers say the focus is tangible! You then ask them to tell their partner what you did.
- Don't forget the power of rhymes and songs for helping us remember things both short and long term. It is not a coincidence that countries all over the world teach young children the alphabet through a song.
- Chunk individual items of information together as often as possible so that instead of eight things to hold on to they have fewer (e.g. bracket similar success criteria together if they are about the same thing/ have a poster of the four things to do at 'Tidy Up Time' then have one signal for tidying up, rather than giving instructions step by step).

The following chapter completes the teaching and learning links, by explaining the impact of 'in-the-moment feedback', both for teachers and especially for children.

12

On-the-move feedback

The good old days

Most of us have memories of many moments in a classroom where either a) you might be asked to answer a tricky question in front of everyone or b) getting on with some independent work and hoping you were on the right track.

I remember having a sneaky look at Michael Bell's work before I started, as he usually knew what he was doing. Whatever the subject, we knew that you'd know how well you'd done, or how much you'd got right if it was a set of maths questions, a comprehension exercise or something similar, once the work had been given in, marked and given back. If you were lucky, you were given time to read the marking comments. It seemed that the expectation was that if you'd listened and focused during the lesson and worked hard, you should be getting everything right.

Feedback, not marking

How things have changed in many schools! 'On-the-move' feedback while children are doing any independent work is now common practice, as we have realised that the greatest impact on children's learning takes place when feedback is given in the moment while the child is engaged in the task rather than afterwards via written comments when it is too late for any misconceptions to be addressed.

DOI: 10.4324/9781003454434-16

Teachers of young children have always been 'on the move' around the classroom, but, as children get older, we've tended to sit back while they work, not wanting to disturb them and only going to children who come for help or put their hands up.

On-the-move feedback tends to have two stages:

1   The first five minutes to check that all are on task and making decisions if there are any problems (e.g. stopping the class if too many children are not sure of what to do or asking learning partners to explain to their partner if only a few are unclear).

2   After all are on track, walking around the room to spot either careless slips (*Just go back and check this spelling/this calculation*) or to have a whispered two-minute conversation at a deeper level (e.g. *What else do you know about multiples that might help you here?/ Could you describe the chaos you said was happening on Christmas morning? Tell us about the presents being opened and what was happening? Tell me what it was like ...*).

In this way, many issues are addressed during the lesson, guiding the children and informing the teacher. Along with other powerful feedback strategies, such as mid-lesson learning stops and co-operative feedback, there is little left for the teacher to 'mark' after school. So, teachers are less anxious, having time to prepare lessons rather than spend inordinate amounts of time marking and now have some precious relaxation time.

Links with attachment theory

It was when Angela watched one of my video clips of 'on-the-move' feedback in Sarah LeTemplier's class of eight and nine-year olds in Clearwater School that she pointed out how linked with attachment theory it was. She said how reassuring it was for children to have Sarah constantly walking around bending down to talk to individual children, often coming back to them. Her physical presence is containing – she is there, with them, answering their needs, making sure they are all ok.

Of course, from a learning point of view, on-the-move feedback means that children don't have to continue with work they are not understanding or getting wrong or sit feeling stuck but worried about sharing that. And, of course, the one-to-one dialogue means that every child has the best scenario for understanding what is being suggested: in context, in the moment, with a chance to ask questions quietly.

Anxiety reduced on every level

On-the-move feedback, therefore, reduces anxiety in two ways: by being a reassuring physical presence and by giving suggestions for improvement or praise for what is being achieved. In Chapter 8, I talked about praising children through a continuous running commentary while they are working, focusing on task or achievement and/or learning behaviour (e.g. *I like the way you have described the feelings he had at being new to the class and jotting down those few ideas on your facing page in your book was a good idea and showed you were planning your words carefully*). This task-related praise (rather than ego-related) makes children feel that it is their application to the task that leads to success, rather than who they are, which has an immediate calming effect. Instead of being constantly compared to others by hearing how clever the teacher thinks certain children are, the child hears that we are all capable of achieving success and making improvements.

> **Anxiety-free learners are in a good position to learn, reinforced by the Maslow pyramid which tells us that children can't think unless they have those needs met, one of which is 'Feeling valued by others and having good self-esteem'.**

13

Curriculum opportunities to discuss emotive themes

Talk is the most effective form of therapy, and classrooms are good places to open up discussions about emotional, often taboo, subjects. Instead of expecting children to discuss their own personal experiences of feelings such as loss, anger, worry and regret, curriculum links provide perfect opportunities to talk about these emotions at a safe distance from children's own lives. By discussing how a character in a novel feels about feeling different, for instance, the focus is on the character, but the resonance is with children in the class who have felt that way. When the teacher asks about strategies for helping the character feel better, the refugee child in the room starts to feel comforted: that it is ok to feel different but that there are more hopeful times ahead.

Integrating opportunities to have discussions as they arise in various school subjects and topics is a way of creating continuity of care for our children rather than having 'bolt-on' lessons or discussions apart from regular lessons. Sarah LeTemplier, from Clearwater Academy in Gloucester, provided us with a number of curriculum links, which other teachers have now added to. These have been organised by subject, as that is how teachers tend to plan. The opportunities are endless, if we are looking out for them.

DOI: 10.4324/9781003454434-17

English and drama	
Emotive themes	**Discussion opportunities (see a list of core texts in the next chapter)**
Loss	Many texts about loss – The Boy in the Tower, The Highwayman, Pog and The Arrival
Anger	Wide exploration opportunities to most texts in a class – character's reaction to something and the reason for their actions
Anxiety and worry	Wide exploration opportunities to most texts in a class – character's reaction to something, the reason for their actions, how normal this is and how people face situations they are worried about.
	Role playing different scenarios and discussing them.
Guilt and regret	Wide exploration opportunities to most texts in a class – also great opportunities to discuss character regret and write about it (diary, letter – link to how this might help all of us).
Feeling different	Wide exploration opportunities to most texts in a class – different characters, ideas, outlooks, appearances, religions and characteristics. Winnie-the-Pooh is great for this (Eeyore = sadness, Piglet = anxiety, Owl = valuing intelligence and feeling aloof, Pooh = always hungry and looking to serve his tummy and Christopher Robin who loves all of his friends for just who they are and allows them space to be who they are without trying to change them).
	'The boy at the back of the class': story about a refugee.
	'Krindlekrax', 'Me and my dad at the end of the rainbow'.

Science	
Emotive themes	**Discussion opportunities**
Loss	Life Cycles (tree, butterfly and dandelion) – how it forms a vital and expected part of life (KS1 (Key Stage 1: five- to seven-year-olds) and KS2 (Key Stage 2: eight- to 11-year-olds)).
Anger	How important figures such a Greta Thunberg has turned anger into positive and polite action.

Science	
Emotive themes	**Discussion opportunities**
Anxiety and worry	Practical science experiments that don't go as hoped or planned can be a great lesson in that things don't always go to plan or our way and that is okay. This is okay in our daily lives too.
Guilt and regret	Materials – irreversible changes. How might this link to our actions?
Feeling different	Studying different plant species – all need different conditions, all look different and all valued and beautiful. This applies to us too. Food chain, our different place in it

History	
Emotive themes	**Discussion opportunities**
Loss	Legacies of important historical figures – how influence, love and 'help' can continue; loss of life in World War II (WWII) and current conflicts.
Anger	Conflicts, wars: why did they start? Poor versus rich people in Victorian times and before. Poverty caused great anger and many protests.
Anxiety and worry	WWII and its impact on people in all countries involved. Current conflicts.
Guilt and regret	What impact have actions from people of the past had? What can we learn from this? Can be linked to actions on our own lives we are not proud of, not necessarily shared or verbalised out loud in class, written or 'imagined' processing (e.g. imagine a conversation where you might want to say sorry – or write and seal a letter that you may not (or may!) send. Draw a picture to show how you would have liked the event to have gone, etc.). Crime and punishment–Vikings and exile. Colonialism, slavery, WWII survivor's guilt, peer pressure on Germans.
Feeling different	WWII and other conflicts: displaced people/Ukraine/channel crossings Windrush generation invited to the UK for work.

Geography	
Emotive themes	**Discussion opportunities**
Loss	Earthquakes/tsunamis/volcanos and their impact (if topical).
Anger	How important figures such a Greta Thunberg has turned anger into positive and polite action.
Anxiety and worry	All of the themes in this section lead to anxiety and worry.
Guilt and regret	Colonialism, slavery, WWII survivor's guilt and peer pressure on Germans.
Feeling different	The world is filled with difference! Cultures, religions, languages and music. Earth is home to billions of people and not one person is the same as another!

Religious education	
Emotive themes	**Discussion opportunities**
Loss	Hinduism: Trimurti – three key deities who represent creation, preservation and destruction – can be linked to life cycles and the importance of destruction, death, etc., through discussion around the seasonal cycle of a deciduous tree, sunrise and sunset and life and death. Reincarnation, Christianity's beliefs about the afterlife.
Anger	King Herod – why was he angry?
Anxiety and worry	(links with loss for this section) How different people (of any or no religion) can be supported by the idea of spirituality. This can be from a simple reflections, stillness and silence to listen to ourselves to really sift our feeling (while trapping out all external influence and noise) to how different people feel supported by established religions and their practices (prayer for a Muslim, Aarti – worship including light in Hinduism).
Guilt and regret	Judas's betrayal, the story of Adam and Eve.
Feeling different	The world is filled with difference! Cultures, religions, languages and music. Earth is home to billions of people and not one person is the same as another!

Music and art	
Emotive themes	**Discussion opportunities**
Loss	Evocation of emotive feelings, how to create sadness using musical instruments and music used on sad occasions.
Anger	Reasons for creations of works to show anger: For example War Requiem, art works portraying anger and releasing anger through drumming and percussion.
Anxiety and worry	The calming effect of music and art: For example the harp, Debussy, impressionism – Monet.
Guilt and regret	Judas's betrayal, the story of Adam and Eve in art, Van Gogh's worries.
Feeling different	Studying quirky ideas from artists and celebrating difference and unique approaches as artistic success (see Tate Modern). Instrumental and sonic differences, music from different cultures taking different forms.

Other opportunities

Loss: Fundraising to raise money for tragic events

PE (physical exercise) avoids the creation of **anger** by ensuring fairness; discussion about fairness in sport (e.g. Maradona hand of God incident, cheating in cycling, etc.

Lunchtime football – how to lose with grace and avoid **anger.**

Cooking: releasing **anger** – kneading bread.

During or after social times of the day: when there has been a disagreement or incident where a child has shown anger – unpicking this and reiterating that all feelings are okay, and it's okay to be angry and discussing strategies to deescalate the anger rather than feed it with adult anger and immediate punishment.

Anxiety –some children have never used public transport.

Guilt and regret: politicians' excuses for breaking rules.

Feeling different discussed as PSHE (personal, social, health and economic education).

What questions should we ask?

The following examples and thoughts about the potential for discussion about WWII provide a model for the kinds of questions teachers might ask, to encourage talk, thinking, empathy and validation. These can be adapted across the curriculum areas.

For a topic on WWII, for instance, which links mainly with loss and maybe guilt, we could ask:

- ◆ *How do you think families felt at the prospect of losing their loved ones? Why do you think that? What would they worry about?*
- ◆ *What advice would you give them if you could help them?*
- ◆ *Why do you think many Germans still feel guilty about the war, even though they are a different generation?*

Sarah added the following thoughts and questions:

When asking the children how they might or do feel about something, it would be worth exploring their responses further, following a line of questioning based on their responses. For example, if they said they would feel anger, you might explore questions such as 'How could people deal with feeling angry when it is because of someone else's action?' This refers back to lack of control and how a person might need to find an outlet for their anger or use it to fuel positive change, for example. We might further ask, for instance:

- *Do you think the soldiers believed in what they were doing? That it was right? (Follow up by questions relating to personal identity, beliefs and purpose).*
- *Once you have done something you regret, what can you do to recover? What kind of actions can you make up for or undo? How would you feel if your action was irreversible? What can a person do if they've done something that they can't change?*

When exploring such themes, I always keep in mind that some children will have felt these or similar experiences, while the vast majority of others will also experience them at some point in the future too. If they have even a very basic understanding of the idea that these feelings are normal, valid and then have understanding of strategies that may help, then our children will be on the road to being equipped to help themselves and others when needed.

Warning! **When embarking on discussions about these emotions, make sure that children are** not asked to reflect on their own personal experiences **but instead stay focused on the situation or characters being discussed.** *What could the soldier do to stop feeling guilty?* **for instance, will help the child examine the issues of conflict solution from a safe distance, subconsciously resonating with their own experience, rather than 'Have you ever felt guilty about hurting someone?' which, as you can imagine, could cause a great deal of angst, embarrassment and public humiliation and actually increase anxiety.**

14

The power of nature and the arts
Music, drama and art

Nature

How do green spaces and nature affect our mental and emotional wellbeing?

We are all part of nature. Our ancestors knew this, but in our modern societies, we can lose sight of it, especially if we live in towns and cities. Yet we all know instinctively that nature is good for us. We need fresh air. It fills not just our lungs but our spirits too. It gives us a sense of being alive. We are emotionally moved in some way when we see a sun setting, a forest, a desert, a seascape and a mountain range; when we smell the sea, bluebells and roses; and when we hear the wind roaring, waves crashing and a bird singing its dawn song. We experience nature through our senses. Our minds do not have to work hard for us to experience it. It is just there.

It has become increasingly clear that nature can offer benefits to people who struggle with mental and emotional health. In the UK, in 2020, a young person with autism, Dara McAnulty, published his diary. He has become well known in the nature world and in the world of autism. We can read how intensely nature helps him in the following extract from his book:

A restful night's sleep is not something I'm familiar with. I find it hard to process and phase out so much of our overwhelming world .... Bright colours cause a kind of pain, a physical assault of the senses. Noise can be

DOI: 10.4324/9781003454434-18

unbearable. Natural sounds are easier to process, and that's all we hear on Rathlin. Here, my body and mind are in a kind of balance. I don't feel like this very often. It means I can reconnect with myself and my family.

McAnulty (2020)

McAnulty is talking about the fact that nature is just there – it is gentle to our senses. We also are just there, just being, but we can lose that inner calm knowledge of ourselves in the midst of our busy and stressful lives. Many of the difficulties McAnulty has experienced are not exclusive to children with autism. The world can be overwhelming when negative emotions are too much for us. Being in nature is a way of finding relief and respite from our busy worlds.

MindUK makes the following claims on its website: *Bringing green spaces and nature into your everyday life can increase mental and physical wellbeing.*

They point to an array of improvements, including the following:

◆ *Improved mood*
◆ *Reduced feelings of stress and anger*
◆ *Improved confidence*
◆ *Improved self-esteem*
◆ *Increased activity*

Biodiversity – empowering children and young people

In Chapter 1, we referred to children's concern about climate change. Schools are essential in facilitating children to grow their knowledge about their natural surroundings. Apart from nature's general mental health benefits, more knowledge about it helps children to feel empowered and more hopeful about their future. They can learn about the biodiversity of all living things on our planet, can be told which species need help to survive and can find ways to act, like helping to create wildlife areas in their gardens and neighbourhoods, or taking part in a school project to help clear local streams and ponds.

As we educate them about their natural world, they will take the knowledge into their adulthoods. We are already seeing this happen, with young people like Greta Thunberg, the 20-year-old Swedish climate activist who has challenged world leaders on their policies. Many are treading a similar path. Mya-Rose Craig, a British-Bangladeshi environmentalist, bird watcher and diversity activist, founded Race Equality in Nature and writes movingly in her book *Birdgirl* about the immense benefits of nature for everyone:

Around a campfire at the end of a successful camp weekend, we would discuss how being outside in nature made us feel, both physically and emotionally. While flames flickered in the dark, we would talk about racism, poverty, issues of identity, how none of these hurdles were going to disappear overnight, but that by engaging with nature, by relishing the fresh air, we were gaining tools to support us and help us cope with everything else life threw at us. This is what was missing from the nature sector: the simple message that nature is good for everyone, but especially those in need.

Craig (2022)

Mya-Rose points to appreciating nature as being an essential tool to mitigate against the many pressing issues that are entering children and young people's worlds today. Nature just makes us feel better; it gives us a sense of peace and calm.

Forest Schools

Many adults who care for and educate children are finding that they can help them to find peace and calm by using 'Forest School.' Children can also find joy and excitement, which are wonderful ways of promoting improved mental health. Schools can access days in nature or camping experiences, depending on the facilities of their local Forest School.

Forest Schools began in Scandinavia. They were seen as embracing an open-air and healthy way of life. They were introduced to the UK in 1993 and grew from strength to strength. They are now practised by trained practitioners all over the world. They foster independence, confidence, self-esteem, creativity and supportive risk taking, all of which are vital for all children but especially so for those with mental or emotional health difficulties.

The following quotes can be found on the Forest School Association website:

Forest School is a feeling you can't put into words.
Tonicha, *aged 9*

I don't have ADHD when I am out in the woods.
David, *aged 14*

After over 15 years working in Forest School, I have had the privilege to watch the pedagogy help selective mute learners find their voice, troubled learners find a more stable path, and watch children at risk of imprisonment because of their behaviour 'singing' with glee whilst sitting on a bench they had made from scratch, using hand tools that they never thought they would be allowed to hold. This is the real power of Forest School.
Nic, *aged 46*

Schools don't have to use Forest Schools, excellent though they are. They can create their own forest school equivalents, which help children to learn to love nature and to feel empowered to help create a healthier world:

A village school situated in a forest can use or create a wooded area bordering its playground, however small, for Forest School activities. These could include discovering wildflowers, insect habitats and building dens.
A primary school on the coast could use the local beach to act out how it would have been to be on the beaches in the Victorian or other eras, what natural hazards would have existed and what wildlife there would have been compared to today.
A primary school in the city could visit its nearest park or city farm, noting the many varieties of trees, flowers and animals and learning about tending the land and animal welfare.
On school trips, late evening walks can be taken, giving children the sense of awe and wonder at the stars in the universe and allowing them to use their senses, listening and looking out for night creatures.
Any school can develop a little patch of land in their playground on which children can grow vegetables and flowers, learning about the whole process from seed to fruit, the cycle of nature and its magic – seeing a tiny seed and imagining the huge plant it can produce can be as awe inspiring as looking at the stars.
Having a bird-watching week, as seen in the photos in Figs. 14.1 and 14.2, where children can see and hear local birds. This sensory experience can then lead to the children drawing the birds, using their memories and perceptions of the birds to enhance their drawings.

 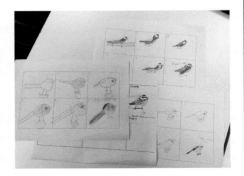

Figure 14.1 Bird watching (six/seven years)   Figure 14.2 Drawing the birds (six/seven years)

By learning within the context of their environment, children are experiencing it first hand; they are learning its importance and how humans are an integral part of nature. They learn this through their senses, allowing their cognitive thinking brains to slow down, which reduces anxiety, can help with depressed feelings and dissipate negative emotions. Children can also see themselves in the context of something bigger; they can feel not helpless but helpful as they nurture areas that encourage more wildlife. Children are our future, and they need to know how much they can offer to the world.

The Arts

Morison, Simonds and Stewart (2021) explored the effectiveness of creative Arts-based interventions on children and adolescents with post-traumatic stress disorder (PTSD). They found that Arts-based interventions significantly reduced symptoms of PTSD and negative mood (i.e. low mood). The interventions included painting or drawing, pottery, sculpture, music, drama, dance, clowning and poetry. They could be implemented individually, in group settings or in a classroom setting. Reasons given for the success of the Arts included their sensory nature. Just as we experience nature through our senses, so we experience the Arts through our senses.

Using our senses and our imaginations

When using our senses, we do not have to think. Instead, we absorb what is in front of us. At a concert or theatre production, in an art gallery, we are absorbing through our senses, which might later promote thoughts and conversations but at the time fill us with the experience. The same process takes place when we create art, in whatever form. If children can perceive an artistic activity through their senses, it promotes calm. Recurring thoughts in anxious or traumatised children will likely reduce whilst doing or watching the Arts.

Further, using our senses fosters our imaginations. When listening to a piece of music, many people have pictures or colours in their heads. Music can inspire imaginative stories and poems. Our ability to imagine, to think and dream beyond what we perceive drives our creativity, which is fundamental to our existence.

How children can use their senses in the Arts to help their emotions – in-the-moment mindful activities

Meditation and mindfulness

Ravi Shankar, an award-winning Indian composer and sitar player, who successfully brought Indian music into Western culture, spoke of his early training when he was delivering a concert and a talk at Bradford Town Hall, UK, in the early 1980s. He said that for the first six months of his training at age 5, he was only allowed to play one note. The learning was in the listening and in the perception of that one note.

This was a lesson in meditation and mindfulness. It is hard to imagine children of today managing that discipline! They can be helped, though, to experience the Arts in a sensory way, using some boundaries and discipline to help to create a receptive mood of calm.

Neuroscience evidence: art and music

The wisdom of Ravi Shankar's teacher was passed down from his ancestors so he knew instinctively how to teach his young student. Today, we have neuroscience to provide evidence for this instinctual knowledge. Lisa Hinz (2020) refers to neuroscience being used to investigate brain structures and functions in operation during artistic processes. In her analysis of this research, Hinz has been able to point to the different emotions and states of mind that can be brought about through various sensory and emotive artistic activities. Some examples are as follows:

Finger painting brings about a sense of calm, focused attention.
Mixing watercolour paint while focusing on the blending of colours has the function of being soothing; using wet brushes and wet, absorbent paper helps the colours to blend easily.
Collage making brings about calm and absorption in the task.
To feel the sensation of clay, to mould a sphere, makes a person focus on their internal thoughts and feelings.
When painting to music, a feeling or mood can be captured in visual form, helping emotions to be labelled and identified.
A group or class singing or humming four notes at the same time, like G, A, B and D, brings about calm and focus; this can be built up slowly from all singing one note initially.
A group or class experimenting with instruments to convey different emotions, such as sadness, happiness, anger, jealousy and confusion, brings about a focus on their internal worlds and helps emotions to be labelled and identified.

These activities all focus on the experience. They can take place in groups or in whole classes. To bring the learning to consciousness, children can share with their learning partners their perceptions and experiences after the activity is completed. This also builds trust and safety in the classroom.

The activities help to develop emotional literacy and can reduce anxiety. They work on different parts of the brain than more structured art or music lessons where more cognitive parts of the brain are developed.

Anecdote

As a young class teacher, I prepared water colours, brushes and paper for each child. I asked them to be quiet as they entered the room in their usual high energy post lunch mood. As they lifted their brushes, an air of calm permeated the room. I was genuinely surprised to see the most disruptive and energetic boy in my class, who needed constant help to focus, completely absorbed when I gave the class ten minutes to just experience the blending of water colours. The time I had spent preparing the lesson was time well spent.

Drama – reaching inside oneself

Acting requires a person to reach inside themselves and to find a way of communicating deep emotions. Actors find that whatever character they are playing will resonate with their own lives and emotions, adding to the authenticity of their performance. It is both a very private and a very public profession. This aspect of acting can be used to help children with mental health difficulties of all kinds to reach inside themselves and can be helpful and relieving.

In acting out different characters, children need to know their own character and how it may differ from the character they are assuming. In the following examples, children are thinking about a particular character and identifying it. In doing this, they are developing their awareness of how human beings operate and how they communicate with each other non-verbally.

In partners, children can guess which character from a given book their partner is acting. They can use their whole bodies to convey the character, then only use their faces, so they have to focus in on the emotion particular characters would express in their facial features. After the exercise, they can discuss which was easier, the whole body or the face exercise.

Children can practice in class or circle time how to look happy, sad, angry, confused, etc. They can then discuss which emotions were easier or harder to spot.

Drama can be developmental

Teachers can individualise how they assign acting roles both in drama lessons and in performances. For understandable reasons, teachers tend to choose children who are confident to play bigger roles and children who are less so to play less exposed roles in drama. If teachers have an awareness of the personalities and attachment styles of particular children in their class (see Chapter 3 *Attachment Styles in the Primary School Context*), they can assign acting roles to children that will be developmental for the children at the same time as producing a good performance. Some examples are as follows:

Shy and avoidant children can hide behind a mask or beard to play larger-than-life characters that can help them to express hidden emotions they normally suppress.
Children who struggle to regulate emotions or who are traumatised can enjoy small but significant parts, where they are popular and loved.
Children who are anxious and sensitive can feel bolder if given roles where they can be independent.

Approached in this way, drama can serve as a useful tool to help children to gain confidence and to feel a valued member of a group. We all want to give parents/carers, friends and relatives a wonderful performance when we invite them to a well-rehearsed play. It is worth remembering that the audience is incredibly forgiving and likely to know not just their own child but also the other children performing. They will thus all be delighted when shy, quiet, avoidant Eva manages to play an assertive, bold part. Someone else in the class might have performed it better, but Eva will touch people's hearts. Drama is a powerful way to help our children to find their true potential.

Teamwork – the Arts help children to work together
Singing together for children and adults

When a group of children sing together, they are in a team. There is no winner or loser but a team of people all co-operating to create a harmonious sound. We don't need extra-curricular choirs to facilitate singing. It can be done in the classroom. There are a wealth of books and online resources with songs for schools, and not to be forgotten are the traditional songs that can reflect the cultures of class members.

> **Anecdote**
>
> *I worked in a school where the more musical teachers were able to teach songs to a group of teachers who felt less confident musically. This became a temporary community choir of educators as and when it was needed. It gave each teacher the confidence to sing with their classes.*

Singing in a containing classroom is less pressured than performing for both children and adults too. Children who struggle with performing can just listen or sing in the chorus while they are sitting in their familiar seat. If a song works well for a class, it could be included in the next concert. With familiarity and association with the classroom, children are more likely to manage a performance. They may find they even enjoy it! Singing is a part of being human. It is not about getting it right or wrong but just giving it a try. It helps children to feel part of a group and to feel responsibility for each other.

Acting together as a cast

> **Anecdote**
>
> *I remember an inspirational teacher who gave our school the experience of acting a production of The Wizard of Oz in our local grand Town Hall. She herself was a member of a successful amateur dramatic company. She brought to us her experience of acting together in a big production. I discovered the camaraderie in the green room behind the stage and the responsibility of turning up on stage at the right time, to make the whole performance work well. We were a team; friendships were forged and we all worked together.*

With such an experience, whether a big or small production, it becomes irrelevant whether you are playing a major or a minor part, for you to learn that every part is key to making the whole production. Children who are less keen on acting or who struggle socially can also work on scenery sets, helping with lighting and marketing – they are all part of the essential team.

Collage making as a team

In the Neuroscience evidence section, I referred to collage making bringing about calm and absorption in the task. It also helps children to work together as a team, thus helping them socially. Children with social difficulties can be helped immensely with group projects where they can take part

Figure 14.3 Four or five years worked together to make a collage of poppies for Remembrance Day

without pressure. Art projects level children's abilities and perceptions of each other. In Fig. 14.3, we see the result of a class of four- to five-year-olds making a group collage of poppies for Remembrance Day. In doing this, they would have had to hold in mind not only their own personal contribution to the collage (i.e. small pieces of paper in particular colours) but also the bigger group picture. This involves taking account of where other children put their pieces of paper and of how the poppies and their surroundings form. It would have required patience, turn-taking, awareness of others, language and structure. The resulting striking piece of artwork is owned by the group, under the guidance of their educators. Thus, the making of a group collage engages complex social abilities and leads to a sense of a pride in their achievements as a class.

Learning from an expert, working as a team and celebrating

The photos in Figs. 14.4 and 14.5 are the result of a class of nine- to ten-year-olds working with an artist to each make a lantern based on the theme of Alice in Wonderland. They then made one big lantern and joined an annual

Figure 14.4 (Nine or ten years) lantern

Figure 14.5 (Nine or ten years) lanterns ready for City Lantern procession making on the theme of Alice in Wonderland

City Lantern procession through the town. This kind of artistic activity gives the children an experience of learning directly from an expert in the field; it allows their creativity to flourish within the context of a theme; it helps them to listen to others, turn-take and work together to create one big lantern; it gives them a sense of being active members of a community and of celebrating with a diverse group of people.

Educators need to use their senses and intuition too

Educators as well as children need to be open and receptive to what they see and hear in their children's artistic activities, to use their senses and intuition to find the moment that builds a young person's confidence and can be potentially life changing. Andria Zafirakou (2023) writes about a student of hers, Jacob, who will not engage with art. He will frequently rip up his work and pronounce himself 'rubbish'. In starting a new project about identity, this teacher invites Jacob to just enjoy the process of painting whatever 'identity' brings to mind. He paints a raw and brilliant piece of art. Andria finds an artist who she is reminded of from the painting and shows this artist's work to Jacob. She writes as follows:

> Jacob realised his work did count and that he was just as entitled to be there as the other students. Some young people feel so isolated and it can some-times take a simple thing, or sometimes it takes a bigger eureka moment, to change this trajectory. As teachers, we don't know what can trigger this, but when it happens we must harness it.
>
> Zafirakou (2023)

Andria remained open to Jacob's ambivalence about art whilst holding onto his potential. She withheld judgement in her words and undoubtedly in her body language. When she saw his painting, she grasped the moment and changed Jacob's whole attitude to art.

Happier, healthier children in nature and the Arts – reaching our potential

If we look at Maslow's Hierarchy of Needs (Fig. 14.6) through a lens of learning about nature and the Arts, we can see that these activities are in every layer of the pyramid; it makes children feel safer in our world; working together gives them a sense of belonging and develops trust; working as a team in nature and the Arts helps them to feel valued by others and raises self-esteem; learning, exploring and being curious about their natural world develop their cognition; nature and the Arts help them to appreciate and accept beauty. Most importantly, by learning about nature and the Arts, children can reach their potential and can grow personally. This is the highest human achievement we can experience; through it, our children become happier, healthier human beings.

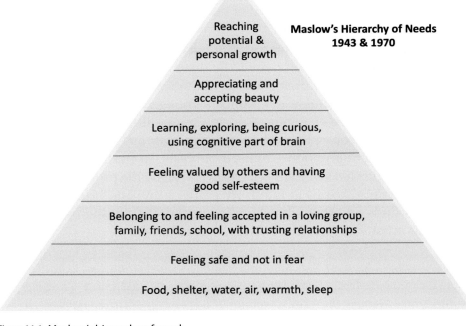

Figure 14.6 Maslow's hierarchy of needs

15

The power of the arts
Using powerful emotive texts to link with learning intentions

Many marvellous children's stories explore difficult emotions, with themes of guilt, bullying, anger, remorse and so on.

We were lucky enough to discover Sarah Le Templier, a Year 4 teacher (eight- to nine-year-olds) from Clearwater Academy in Gloucester, who is skilled at not only using texts to explore difficult emotions but also to use model texts from books such as those listed to link with literacy learning intentions. Sarah's words are in purple italics throughout this chapter, as she takes us through her strategies and some example lessons.

Case study: Sarah Le Templier's use of texts

I believe that high-quality books really are the best drivers to explore different people, experiences and situations and hence explore emotions that might resonate with us (books as 'mirrors') and emotions that might help us to learn and understand more (books as 'windows'). If you're using high-quality books for reading, this offers expressive responses from the children in the form of writing. This can be both emotionally educational and therapeutic, and often leads to really good writing.

DOI: 10.4324/9781003454434-19

We predominantly use our core texts (see the list) to help to explore emotive themes, particularly loss, anxiety, shame, in fact any feeling that can be explored via characters or circumstances. We integrate this into our writing and discussion on a daily basis.

In all of our class texts, in every circumstance any of the characters find themselves experiencing, we always talk about all feelings being okay and are normal (e.g. if a character is angry, anxious or heartbroken – as well as seemingly positive emotions), but our actions have huge significance on ourselves and others around us.

Core texts at Clearwater School, used for exploring emotive themes

Y3 (7/8 yrs.)   **Y4 (8/9 Yrs.)**   **Y5 (9/10 yrs.)**   **Y6 (10/11 yrs.)**

Y3 The Miraculous Journey of Edward Tulane by Katie Dicamiilo – loss and recovery.

Y3 Varjak Paw by S F Said – survival.

Y4 Kensuke's Kingdom – loneliness, anger, judgement, anxiety and worry.

Y4 The Iron Man by Ted Hughes- regret, judgement, fear, anxiety and worry.

Y4 The Boy at the Back of the Class by Onjali Q Rauf – fear, loss, separation, prejudice, bereavement, anxiety and worry and anger.

Y4 The Last Bear by Hannah Gold – feelings of insignificance, loneliness, loss and love.

Y5 Wonder by R J Palacio – being different, acceptance, bullying, rejection, regret and anger.

Y5 Floodland by Marcus Sedgewick – bullying and bereavement.

Y5 Letters from the Lighthouse by Emma Carroll – prejudice, tolerance and bereavement.

Y5 The Explorer by Katherine Rundell – survival.

Y5 The Girl Who Stole an Elephant by Nizrana Farook – the nature of right and wrong.

Y6 Pig-Heart Boy by Malorie Blackman – love, loss, renewal and betrayal.

Y6 War Horse by Michael Morpurgo – loss, grief, anger, pain and revenge.

Y6 The Girl of Ink and Stars by Kiran Millwood Hargrave – sacrifice and redemption.

Y6 The Other Side of Truth – truth, sacrifice and redemption.

Y6 Can You See Me? By Libby Scott and Rebecca Westcott – valuing differences, acceptance and identity.

Some of these titles could be appropriate to span across a couple of year groups – for example Varjak Paw could be Year 3 or 4. Most of the Y5 texts could also be appropriate for Year 6.

I would add to Clearwater School's core books the following titles:

Y2 Ruby's Worry (a small worry grows until it overwhelms Ruby; it goes away when she shares it with a friend who also has a worry)

Anxiety, friendship, communication, problem solving and the power of sharing feelings

Y6 The Arrival by Shaun Tan (a graphic novel telling the story of a war torn country and the father's journey to start a new life in another country)

Feelings of being lost, frightened or confused in an unfamiliar environment

Y6 A Monster Calls by Patrick Ness (a bereaved boy has repetitive nightmares and wakes to find a monster calling to him)

Grief, family and overcoming suffering

Examples of how Sarah used two of the texts with literacy learning intentions

'The Iron Man' by Ted Hughes
The iron man is a giant who everyone is scared of as he eats everything metal. He is trapped by the neighbours who plan to bury him alive. Hogarth, a child, helps the Iron Man eventually save the world.

One set of three lessons now follows:
NB. Children are thoroughly immersed in the text of the moment, through a daily read, so there is high engagement. They are free to apply the rules

of grammar, punctuation and so on in any of their writing. The lesson is focused primarily around the literacy learning intention, but the necessary discussion about the character's emotions and actions are capitalised on during the analysis and teaching. Not only does this allow for difficult emotions to be explored from an objective point of view, it also enhances the children's understanding of the author's intent and impact on the reader.

We explored Hogarth's fear and actions and used our school values as a moral compass to discuss how ethical his actions are. After Hogarth hints at regret for his actions at the end of Chapter 2, we took this as a stimulus to explore those feelings in a letter addressed to his father.

Learning intention: use expanded noun phrases using nouns to describe feelings

Context: Hogarth's regret and fear, and difficulty expressing his feelings face to face

---

At the end of our reading session, and in preparation for the next lesson, we spoke about how writing uncomfortable feelings down can really help us to process and communicate effectively and fully, without interruption, distraction or persuasion. Without insisting that children lean on experiences in their discussion, children did start to use their own examples of when they might have found it useful to write their thoughts and feelings down, even if it wasn't in a letter to anyone.

We also explored the complexity of being a child and talking to a parent about something that the child isn't proud of (and might fear their thoughts or actions would be frowned upon) and the class was brilliant and forthcoming in talking about the benefits of writing a letter, or even just writing it down, rather than saying it.

After the class discussion, I gave the children two versions of the letter the boy might have written to his father (Figs. 15.1 and 15.2), to examine what an excellent one might look like compared to a good example. We analysed the difference between them and talked about expanded noun phrases.

The children then wrote their own versions of the letter, using expanded noun phrases to describe their feelings. One example of a child's letter, in character, can be seen in Fig. 15.3.

This typical example shows how powerfully the children have been able to describe emotions vicariously while in role as Hogarth, expressing remorse, guilt and putting themselves in the giant's shoes.

Version 1

Dear Dad,

I have something to tell you but I don't really know how to say it. I thought it would be easier to write it in a letter **filled with all of my thoughts**, than tell you face-to-face, as this way I know I will tell you everything that I want to tell you and I won't back down or change my mind.

After what we did to that monster, I have felt a **huge sense of guilt** and I simply cannot shake it off. Don't get me wrong, I know this **grotesque beast** most likely poses great danger for everyone who lives here. We were probably right to stop it in its tracks, but I just feel like such a bully for treating him the way we did, the way I did. Do you think we should have given the **poor thing** a chance before we lured it into our **wicked trap**? The thing is, I do think there is more to this giant and I think we were just terrified of the sheer size of his **colossal body with those raging eyes.** I am beginning to suspect that is wasn't rage we saw, it was desperation.

What if this poor soul was actually looking for help? What if he was climbing up to us in desperation and all we did was entice him into the unforgiving earth, forever buried and never to be seen again.

What did we do Dad? Were we wrong?

I'll see you later and maybe we could talk about this.

Hogarth x

Figure 15.1 Good example 1 of Hogarth's letter

Version 2

Dear Dad,

I have something to tell you but I don't know how to say it. I thought it would be easier to write it in a letter **filled with my thoughts**, than tell you face-to-face.

After what we did to that monster, I have felt a **huge sense of guilt** and I simply cannot shake it off. Don't get me wrong, I know this **grotesque beast** is dangerous for everyone who lives here. We were probably right to stop it but I just feel like such a bully for treating him the way we did, the way I did. Do you think we should have given the **poor thing** a chance before we lured it into our **wicked trap**? I do think he might not be here to hurt us. I think we were just terrified of the size of his **colossal body with those raging eyes.** I am beginning to suspect that is wasn't rage we saw, it was desperation.

What if this poor soul was actually looking for help? What if he was climbing up to us in desperation and all we did was entice him into our trap?

What did we do Dad? Were we wrong?

I feel so bad.

Hogarth x

Figure 15.2 Good example 2 of Hogarth's letter

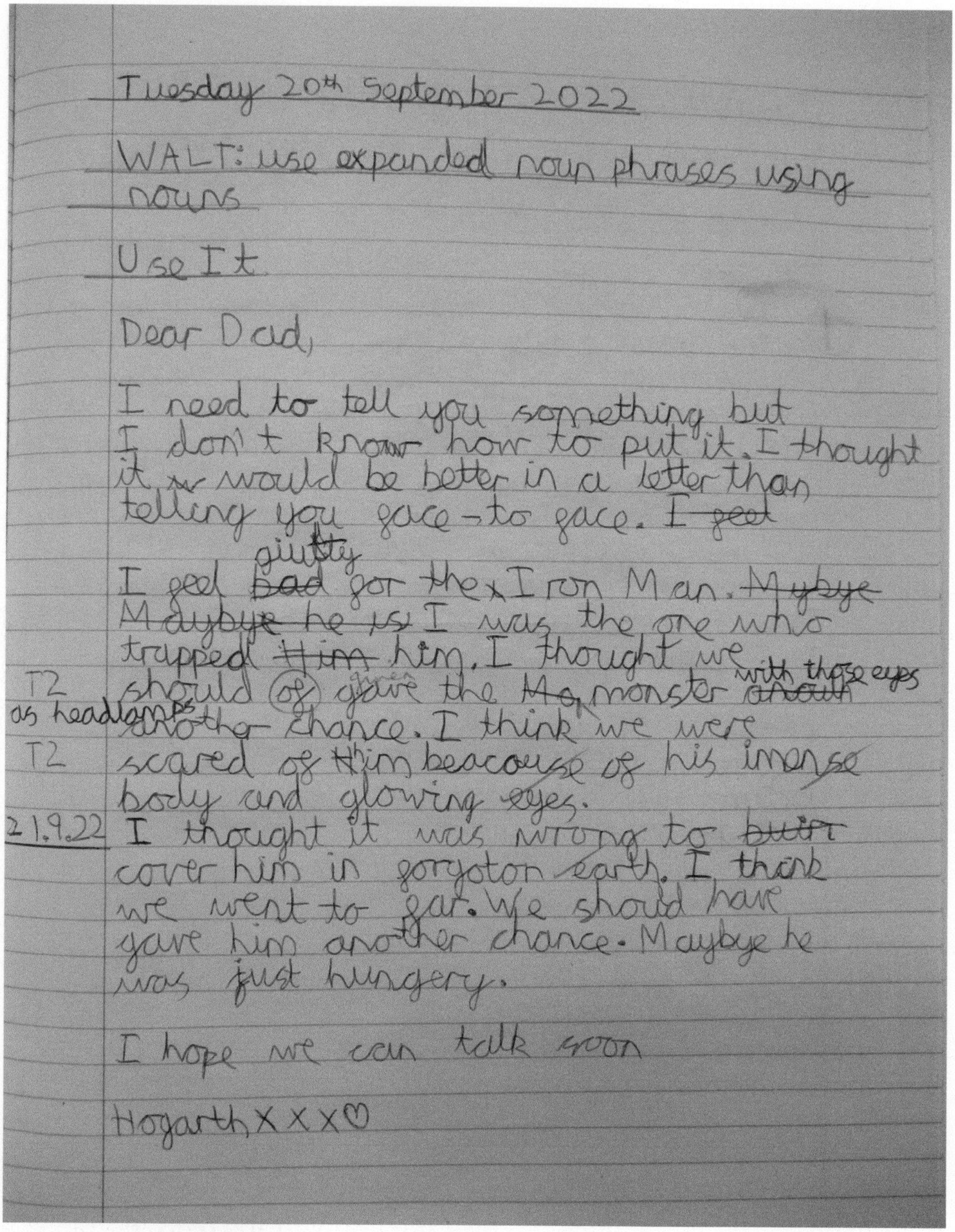

Tuesday 20th September 2022

WALT: use expanded noun phrases using nouns

Use It

Dear Dad,

I need to tell you something but I don't know how to put it. I thought it would be better in a letter than telling you face-to face. I feel

I feel bad for the Iron Man. Maybye he is I was the one who trapped Him him. I thought we with those eyes
T2 should of gave the monster
as headlamps another chance. I think we were
T2 scared of him beacouse of his imense body and glowing eyes.
21.9.22 I thought it was wrong to cover him in gorgoton earth. I think we went to far. We should have gave him another chance. Maybye he was just hungery.

I hope we can talk soon

Hogarth, X X X ♡

Figure 15.3 Child's letter, as Hogarth

Dear mrs letemplier,

I just want to tell you that I am a bit sad. Because of something that happend at the end of break lunch and I got blamed of something I didn't do. So I was playing with [redacted] and we lined up and [redacted] said he was going to tell me of for nothing.

from [redacted]

ps: I didn't want to tell you in person.

Figure 15.4 The first letter (transcribed, exactly as written, for legibility)

Impact!

By coincidence, one week after this lesson on the power of writing a letter, I received this email from Sarah:

A child who had previously had friendship issues looked upset at the end of lunch. I asked if she was okay and she unconvincingly nodded. I offered for her to speak to me any time if I could help with anything. About 10 minutes later the first letter (Fig. 15.4) arrived on my desk.

After reading this, I was able to discreetly talk to the child who wrote it and we agreed that I would talk to everyone involved. It turns out that it had all been a misunderstanding and that everyone felt a bit confused and hurt by the apparent upset. All three smiles returned immediately and they all had a great afternoon in class.

At the end of the day I received a second letter (Fig. 15.5).

I am glad we had discussed the power of writing uncomfortable feelings down in letters the week before!

'The Boy at the Back of the Class' by Onjali Q Rauf

A refugee child from Syria arrives at a UK school and writes about his experiences

Three literacy learning intentions now follow, for three separate lessons, in which there is a dual purpose: enabling discussion about the emotions experienced in the book but also linking with the required literacy curriculum.

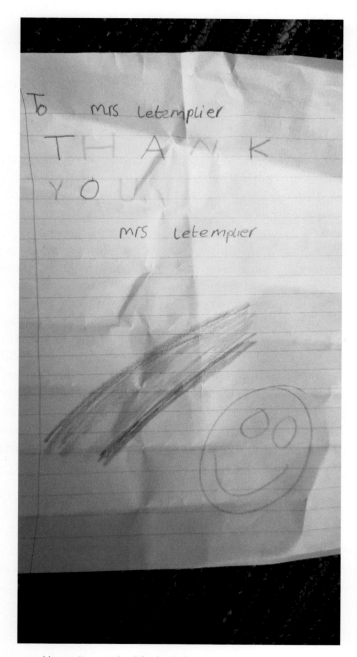

Figure 15.5 The second letter (transcribed for legibility)

Lesson 1 (three sessions)

> **Learning intention: write narrative to infer character**
>
> Context: Ahmet's feelings of being alone in unfamiliar, frightening circumstances on his first day at school

Our end of unit 'Big Write', when we study this book, consists of us putting ourselves in Ahmet's shoes and writing a recount of his first day at a UK school after fleeing the Syrian war and getting displaced from his parents and everyone he knows. He doesn't know the language, he is terrified, confused, exhausted and in desperate need of comfort. We explore those feelings in class and while we haven't had any refugees in our class, we have children who have been displaced, children who experience anxiety and children who can feel out of place. Through our exploration of Ahmet, children felt seen and supported by a familiar notion and were able to share their experiences. I gave them an example of what a good recount might look like which we analysed and discussed (see Fig. 15.6).

The following example (see Fig. 15.7) of an excerpt of one child's recount from this lesson is from a high achieving writer. All the children, however, were able to lose themselves in describing how Ahmet must have felt.

This lesson really supports our context, as it would for many other schools, because we regularly have new children starting and joining Clearwater, so it brings a new level of empathy, understanding and recognised feelings to the surface.

Lesson 2 (three sessions)

> **Learning intention: use speech marks and surrounding punctuation**
>
> Context: A child talks to his mother about Ahmet, developing empathy and understanding of someone else's suffering

I used the part in the book in which a conversation takes place between a child and their mother about the new boy in the class, to lead to a retelling of that dialogue, using speech marks and appropriate punctuation.

We first discussed the importance of how to broach conversations on sensitive subjects. Children can be fearful that they are asking inappropriate questions which might offend but we would like to find out more

---

<u>Good example</u>

I had only been in the building a matter of minutes. Before I knew it, a kind lady called 'Mrs Sanders' took me to where I needed to be but where I really didn't want to go. My new classroom.

Peering from behind her, I saw it all. The gigantic room was filled with children about my age and they all looked the same. They were wearing the same clothes and they even all wore a similar expression on their faces. Those eager faces were all staring straight at me. My throat was dry and tight as I stood there motionless looking at the floor. I wanted it to swallow me up so I could hide from all of these people.

We entered the classroom and dread swept through me. A blanket of sweat washed over me like a wave and I froze.

Another lady, my teacher I think, said, "Everyone, this is Ahmet and he will be joining our class from today." The whole class erupted into mutters and murmurs. Obviously, I had no idea what they were saying but their faces didn't look happy, so I can only imagine that what they were saying was bad.

Within seconds, she held my shoulders and led me over to the one chair that was empty, right at the back of the class. My insides shrivelled with embarrassment as everyone's eyes followed me all the way to my seat. I tried to hide the fact that my entire body was tense and my hands were shaking and I think I did okay at this. Or at least I hope so.

Next to me, there was a quiet girl and her eyes were like daggers and she had a tight bun wound neatly on the top of her head. It was crystal clear that she did not want a partner today. Not me, anyway.

I twitched nervously as her scowl only got worse as I sat there. In front of me, the rest of the class seemed to settle while the teacher continued with whatever lesson they were doing but not this girl, she wanted me gone.

With a sly smirk spreading across her face, she reached for her workbook and held it up like a barrier between us so that she couldn't see me anymore. As much as I tried to tell myself that this is okay, at least I couldn't see her anymore, my heart sank and fear choked me as I realised that this place too wasn't going be so easy.

"Please no," I silently prayed, hoping that this wasn't how life was going to be. I had already been through so much.

I had never felt so rejected.

Figure 15.6 Good example

to help clarify their own understanding. This particular writing related to asking about refugees in the book but it could also be applicable to many topics such as racism, sexual orientation and identity questions, climate change, school safety in the US after seeing news reports and war/displacement ... to name just a few. When we discussed it in class, we kept it really age appropriate but this could form the bedrock of confidence for

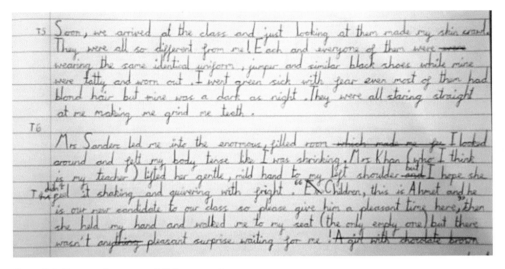

Figure 15.7 Excerpt from one child's recount

more complex questions children might later encounter and are potentially fearful or unsure on how to ask about them.

The storyteller's imagined conversation with their mum is all about developing empathy by noticing and trying to understand difficulties others face. At this point in the story, the children didn't know that the new boy was a refugee or that he didn't speak English – all they knew was that he didn't talk to anyone. We discussed that when someone acts in an odd way, there is always a reason for it, no matter how rude and dismissive it can feel.

I shared two good examples first (see Figs. 15.8 and 15.9), analysing and discussing the content and the punctuation.

A typical example of the children's attempts at this difficult conversation between a boy and his mother can be seen in Fig. 15.10.

Lesson 3 (three sessions)

> **Learning intention: use possessive pronouns**
> **Context: Actions of a bully, exploring anger and normal feelings being expressed**

We used the chapter in the book in which a kind child brings in a pomegranate for Ahmet. The class bully steals the pomegranate and throws it around, until it eventually bursts.

Good example 1

I followed Mum into the kitchen and watched her get out the cocoa jar and switch on the kettle. Then before I knew it, I asked, "Mum, what's a Refugee Kid?"

I didn't really mean to blurt it out like that, but sometimes my mouth does things my brain isn't ready for.

Mum stopped what she was doing and stared at me. "A refugee kid?" she asked, with a frown on her face. "Where did you hear those words?"

"At school," I said. "Someone called the new boy in our class a Refugee Kid."

"You've got a new boy in your class?" I nodded. "And Mrs. Khan didn't tell you anything about him?"

I shook my head. "Only that his name's Ahmet and he's never been to London before. I'm trying to be his friend, but he doesn't talk to anyone, so I can't tell if he wants to be friends too…."

"I see…." Mum fell silent. She poured the milk into the saucepan and waited for it to heat up. I knew she was thinking about something serious because she was rubbing her chin a lot. Mum only ever rubs her chin when she is about to say something serious.

Figure 15.8 Good example 1

Good example 2

When I arrived home from school that day, I couldn't shake the feeling that Ahmet wasn't okay and I didn't really know what I could do to help him.

Mum breezed into the room, cupping a hot mug of tea in her hands. "Hi Love," she said, leaning against the doorframe. "How was school?"

At first I wasn't sure whether or not to tell her about the lemon sherbet incident. Giving the new boy an old, fuzzy sherbet isn't exactly the most heroic thing I've ever done.

"Funny you should ask," I replied. "There is a new boy called Ahmet in my class and I think he's finding it hard to make friends. I tried to speak to him today but I didn't get very far."

A look of pure confusion grew on her face. "What do you mean, you didn't get very far?" she asked, edging closer into the room.

"Well, he hasn't really spoken. Not to me or to anyone else," I mumbled. By this point, I knew I was sounding offended, as if he had been rude to me but he hadn't. I had to explain more. "I don't think he can talk, Mum. It must be so hard for him."

Figure 15.9 Good example 2

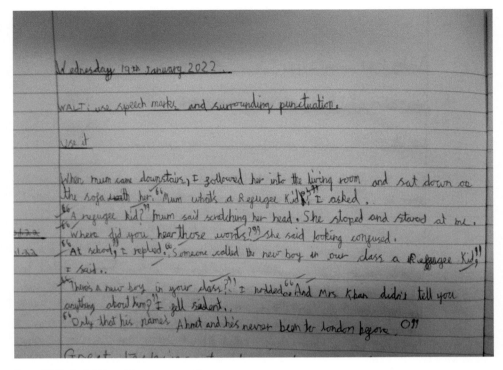

Figure 15.10 A child's written conversation

The retelling of the pomegranate argument is all about naming feelings and understanding that all feelings are normal and okay – even those that are deemed 'negative' or are often encouraged to be supressed (anger, fear, anxiety, embarrassment etc.) We explored anger through the retelling of this scene and paid close attention to how anger can physically make you feel inside, always reassuring that everyone feels this at some point and this is normal and not a negative reflection of whoever is feeling it. When the children wrote their own versions of this, most were able to use their own experiences to create that sensory description which enabled discussion on how we can sometimes feel and what we can do when we feel that way.

We reflected on what we would and could do as the storyteller (they only find out her name at the end, and everyone assumes it's a boy until the very end too!) is confronted and targeted by the bully and also what the role of bystanders could be here. It helped us to unpick what bullying is as opposed to an unkind incident and explore how much unkindness and bullying can cause harm to those who experience it.

Good example

Suddenly, Brendon-the-Bully pushed past us.

"Gimme that!" he barked, snatching the pomegranate from Ahmet's hands.

"Give that BACK!" I shouted, feeling scared and angry at once. I could feel the blood rush to my reddening face.

"Make me!" sneered Brendan-the-Bully as he turned around to face me. Without breaking his gaze, he stepped further towards me.

When someone you don't like looks straight at you, they suddenly seem to grow taller and taller and you feel as if you're getting smaller and smaller. Even though I knew we were really both the same size.

I was feeling so hot and angry that I could feel my ears going red but I didn't care. I took a step forward and tried to grab the pomegranate back.

"Go on, try again!" laughed Brendan-the-Bully, as he whipped it away and held it high above his head. I could feel my face burning crimson as I tried to jump and snatch it back from him.

Figure 15.11 Good example of the retelling

We analysed and discussed the good example of the retelling (see Fig. 15.11) which I shared with the class first.

The two examples of children's subsequent writing (Figs. 15.12 and 15.13) reflected the passion of their feelings in our class discussion.

The use of core texts linked with literacy learning intentions seems not only doable but also rich in outcomes at every level. Teachers have always read children texts which are often full of emotion, but one of the key strategies for helping children to be less anxious is to be more explicit about the emotions which unfold in a story, stopping to ask questions about characters' motives, asking what they could have done differently, putting ourselves in their shoes, expressing empathy and encouraging understanding and kindness. Texts also allow us to explore and normalise emotions such as anger, and how it is ok to feel anger at unfair treatment or circumstances, so that children don't feel that they should be stifling valid emotions to appear to be a better person.

I remember hearing of a nine-year-old child (from another school) who was bullied at school by a so-called best friend and could only ask the bully *What can I do to make you happy?* It was only through therapy that the child was able to express much-needed anger at how she had been treated, mocked in front of other classmates and so on. Once the anger was seen as helpful, the child was able to take more control of the situation then and thereafter.

Thursday 3rd February 2022

WALT: use possessive pronouns

Use it:

T5 In the playground, Brendon took the pomegranate out of Ahmet's

T8 palms. Suddenly he shouted "Your never going to get this back!" with a michivious grin.

T6 Feeling angry and scared at once I screamed "Give that back!!!" to Brendon. At this moment I could feel the anger filling my face.

T9 "Make me!" he sneared. His sneere was as evil as a super villans. He stepped towards me like he was a giant with really bad breathe. His gaze was never brocken.

When someone you don't like doesn't break their gaze at you it feels like there getting taller and your getting smaller.

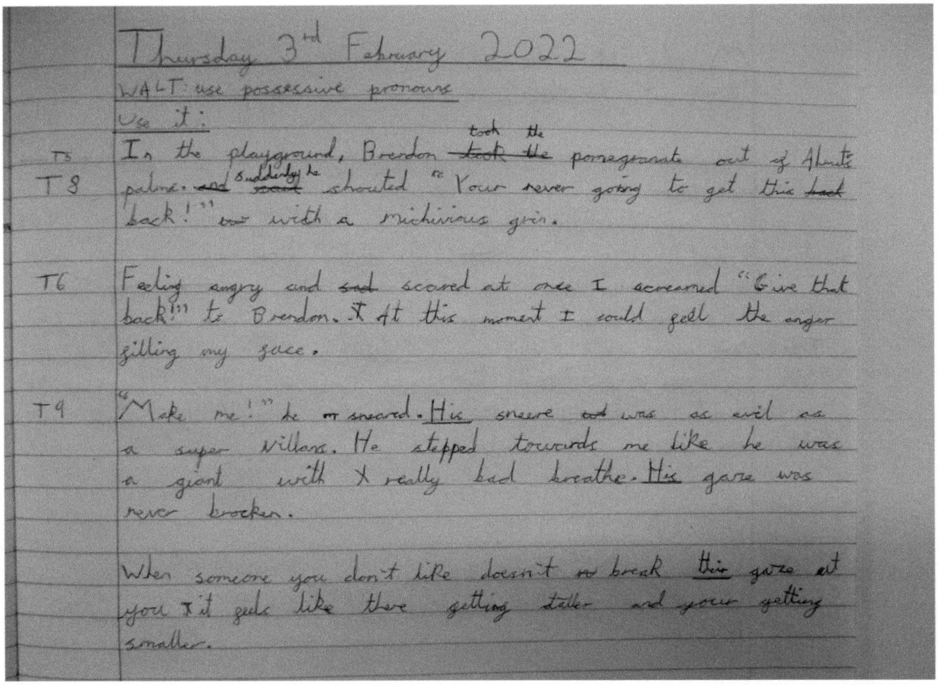

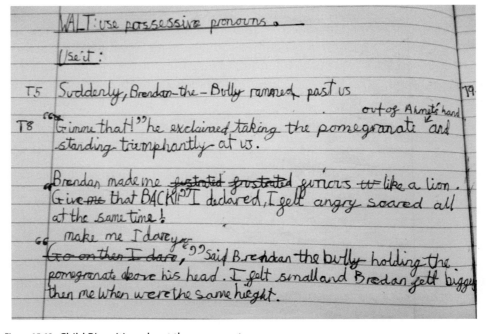

Figure 15.12 Child A's writing about the argument

WALT: use possessive pronouns.

Use it:

T5 Suddenly, Brendan-the-Bully ramned past us

T8 "Gimme that!" he exclaimed taking the pomegranate out of Ahmet's hand and standing triumphantly at us.

Brendan made me frustrated furious like a lion. "Give that BACK!!" I declared, I felt angry scared all at the same time!

"make me I dare you" said Brendan the bully holding the pomegranate above his head. I felt small and Bredan felt bigger then me when were the same hieght.

Figure 15.13 Child B's writing about the argument

Hopefully, by capitalising on the opportunities presented in the kinds of texts, experiences and lessons described in this chapter and Chapters 13 and 14, we can help our children take more control over their emotions, to understand them and to manage them.

PART IV

Creating a containing and compassionate school

16

Visions and values

In this chapter, Kate takes us through her journey of setting up a new school and the lengths to which she went to ensure that her vision and subsequent values were as authentic as possible. She makes the point that there is no right way to set up a school's vision and values, but, nevertheless, the process described here could be helpful to new school leaders, whether a new or already established school. The vision and values creates the foundation for not only the ethos of the school, but also for discussion and dialogue. The values are constantly referred to in the school when discussing any aspect of behaviour and how we should all aim to treat each other. Kate's background of therapy, in various settings, is tangible in her description of her aims and strategies.

My preparation

Excitement, dread and fear

When I set up my own school from scratch, I was given an amazing opportunity, a once in a lifetime opportunity, and an incredibly challenging one.

Imagine taking possession of a building that is completely empty, no infrastructure, no staff, no furniture – absolutely nothing. This filled me with hope and excitement but also quite a bit of trepidation.

Determining my vision

The situation was simultaneously exhilarating and take-my-breath-away scary. There was no existing culture, no ethos; it was the epitome of a blank

DOI: 10.4324/9781003454434-21

page. Everything was truly my responsibility. There can be no blaming an earlier head or senior leadership team, no excusing the culture as something that I had inherited. So, the question I had to face was how to create something from nothing?

I had to think long and hard about the sort of place I wanted it to be. I came up with key areas to focus on; obviously first and foremost the children and their education were the main priority but for them to flourish, what other elements needed to be in place? And how would I ensure that everyone bought into this? I had a vision for the school, but as so often happens, this was more a visual mental image, an imagining at this stage. The challenge was taking the dream that was living in my mind, unpicking it so that others could understand it and turning it into a reality not just for children but for staff and families too. For me I was clear that I wanted my school to be a place of psychological safety, not only for the children but for the adults too.

Modelling the vision

In an earlier setting, I had inherited a team that was in crisis. Despite having a specific Christian vision, this was a place where staff, pupils and families were openly hostile to one another. So, because of this experience I had very definite ideas about what I didn't want it to be. Shockingly, senior staff would ignore specific teachers, refusing to say good morning or reply to a question. Is it any wonder that in this situation the children were rude and unruly? After all they were following the 'vision' being modelled right in front of them. On arrival, I was aware that people did not feel safe or contained. Emotions ran high and unhappiness was apparent. This was a very formative experience and underlined to me that whatever our age, emotional safety and containment is worth investing in. I could 'see' how things could be different, but the challenge was translating my mental picture into a tangible lived experience.

I am sure many of you reading this have found yourselves in similar situations

A vision must be meaningful. At its most effective it ensures the direction of travel for an organisation; it unites a community with a shared understanding and a striving towards a core purpose and hopefully this is underpinned by a contained, safe environment.

Leadership responsibilities

Building Blocks 1 and 2: vision for the school and vision for myself

There are a variety of ways to decide upon a vision. Once set it then needs to be revisited periodically to ensure it is still doing its job. However, for me there are two parts to a successful vision; there is the question of *What will my vision for my school be?* But the other question, one that to me needs to be considered before setting wider aims is: 'What is my vision of myself as a leader/teacher?'

What will my vision for my school be?
What is my vision of myself as a leader/teacher?

I wonder how much time we invest in these key questions for ourselves? Time is rightly spent looking at how to optimise learning in a classroom, how to ensure environments meet our pupils' varying needs, how to budget effectively but we often don't invest in much exploration of ourselves. Yet research shows that the success of an organisation is dependent on those with leadership responsibilities. A project by the National College for Leadership of Schools and Children's Services (2009) found that improved pupil outcomes were attributable to the leaders' values, virtues, dispositions, attributes and competencies.

Some of us might have spent time looking at different leadership styles, or personality types. We might have a notion of ourselves as task driven, or completer/finishers, as an ideas person or as a person who requires time to think before responding. All these descriptions are valid and can help us to know ourselves better. The difficulty is that they don't always explain the 'how' of our behaviour. That is, the impact of our behaviour on others and on their effectiveness, their feelings of safety and security. For example, if we are a task driven, completer/finisher, what vibes are we giving off when we focus on completing a task? Is there an element of tension that others feel? Do we snap at people if they interrupt? Or do we greet their query with a smile and ask them to return at a more convenient time?

Anecdote

I remember a morning when I was phenomenally busy, preparing for an imminent inspection. There appeared at my door two members of staff with a hedgehog in a plastic bag. They had found the hedgehog in the car park and decided to bring it to me. I really did not have the rehoming of a hedgehog on my priority list that day! Several thoughts went through my mind, a pang of irritation, I wondered 'why would anyone put a living creature in a plastic bag?' I thought 'what on earth am I meant to do with a hedgehog?' and 'I really haven't got time for this!'

So, I wonder what your response would've been? A dismissive reply or a warm one? In both situations we can justify our actions, in both situations there will be an impact on a colleague or child, but one will result in a more harmonious working environment for all. So how can we start to understand ourselves better and hold ourselves to greater account for our leadership behaviours?

When faced with what I perceive to be irritating interruptions, whether they involve hedgehogs or humans, I remember my core value 'everyone is important' and try to act according to this. For me that means allowing time to listen.

In this instance it meant we chuckled, we jointly rolled our eyes at the absurdity of the situation and then I passed the problem back to them. 'What would they like to do?' They said they would do some research leaving the hedgehog with me until they had a solution.

This approach had the same outcome as if I'd got cross but with one vital difference, my colleagues felt heard, they had permission to seek a solution, and we all had a giggle. In this situation by actively using a core value as a guide, a potentially irritating moment was dealt with effectively for all.

Personal values

So, to return the question of **What sort of person or leader do you want to be?**, the starting point is always our personal values. I know that looking inwards at our own values is a beneficial building block towards crafting our vision of ourselves. This self-knowledge also gives understanding when our reaction to others grates or brings an unexpectedly strong adverse reaction from us, especially important when we are responsible for a whole school culture. Through a developed understanding of our self we can learn to manage these and in the process provide a place of safety for those we work with. Most of us will at some time or another have considered what is important to us. Many of us will say integrity, honesty or perhaps kindness is important. Often family is a top priority. Most of us would say that we act in accordance with our values, however, I think spending a deeper amount of reflection on what we truly value and then unpicking the detail in terms of what this actually means for our actions and behaviours, pays dividends in the long run and is the second building block for a vision of oneself in action.

Strategies

Activity 1

I would like to suggest an activity to support the building of these two blocks. I first came across this type of activity through my work with Professor Steve Peters. It can be done by yourself but is most effective with a trusted friend or colleague. Take a set of value cards, these can be easily downloaded from the internet, or you can buy a pack. Taking each card one by one you sort through the whole pack. For each card you ask, 'is this a guiding value for me?' You then put it into one of three piles. The first pile is a yes, the second pile a no and the third a maybe. Once you have been through the whole pack you discard your 'no's', put the yeses and maybes together and begin the sorting into three piles again. This is where your friend comes in. It becomes far more challenging to sort at this point, so having a friend to discuss what pile you are going to put a particular card in, when you're hesitating over a choice, is very beneficial. You are then articulating what is or isn't important to you and why. This process is repeated until you have refined your choices to six core values. Along the way will have been rich discussions about the nuances of your own approach to life, the meaning you attach to different values, what is and is not important and where one value may conflict with another. Once this sorting has been done, you have a guide to your behaviour and response to others, particularly helpful when faced with tricky situations, as they act as a reference point.

If we are unclear about our own values, we cannot expect others to be clear about what we stand for. If there is a lack of clarity or a disconnect between what we say our values are and what we actually do, there will be a disconnect with our vision too. It will be hollow. Life will also be more stressful as we will experience cognitive dissonance, the stressful inner jangling that comes from believing one thing and doing the complete opposite.

Building block 3: what it looks like in action

A third building block is needed, once you have elicited your values, on *what does this look like in action?* This does not require your friend unless you wish to complete the whole thing together. A mind map can then be created with the key points on it for you, an aide memoire. For those of you familiar with a dual coding map this will also work, with key words and pictures to illustrate your values and actions in given situations.

I have created a quite simple A4 sheet and look at it regularly; in fact, the sheet itself has disintegrated through overuse. It includes phrases that are meaningful to me and quotes I have read that particularly resonate. Luckily, I took a picture of it (see Fig. 16.1) and when I feel the signs of stress building, I take it out and remind myself of what's truly important. It has a steadying effect, grounding me and supplying a vital support in decision making.

You can provide the same support to your friend for steps one and two of the above process, being a sounding board as they search for what brings meaning to their life. A by-product of completing this with another person is that you gain a true insight into how personal values are and how they have been formed through different yet equally valid experiences. This insight serves us well when faced with people, staff, parents or governors who hold highly differing views. It helps us to accommodate and understand these.

The most helpful part of holding ourselves accountable to our values is that it frees us up from fear of judgement. If we know in our hearts that we have acted according to our values, we have nothing to fear. We also understand that when others disagree, this is not a personal attack on us, but stems from the other person seeing and having experienced the world differently. In fact, it stimulates curiosity and the chance to explore another view. Our anxiety will be less likely to be triggered when we find ourselves faced with strong opposing views or scrutiny. Having answered the questions of *what is my vision of myself as a leader?* and *how will I live this day-to-day?* we now have some firm foundations on which to build and are in a stronger position to provide a containing work environment for others.

Talking to other heads

I spoke to several Head teachers about what they have done when setting a school vision and whilst it is agreed that there is not one 'correct' way and that there are many ways to approach this some common threads appeared. The first was the importance of the vision being based on shared values. Next was the agreement that this process takes time and is best not rushed. Finally, the importance of the team buying into and then striving for the vision was also present.

So there is a 'which comes first the chicken or the egg?' conundrum about setting a vision. A working team needs clarity of vision but again it will only be successful if people are clear about the values, culture and

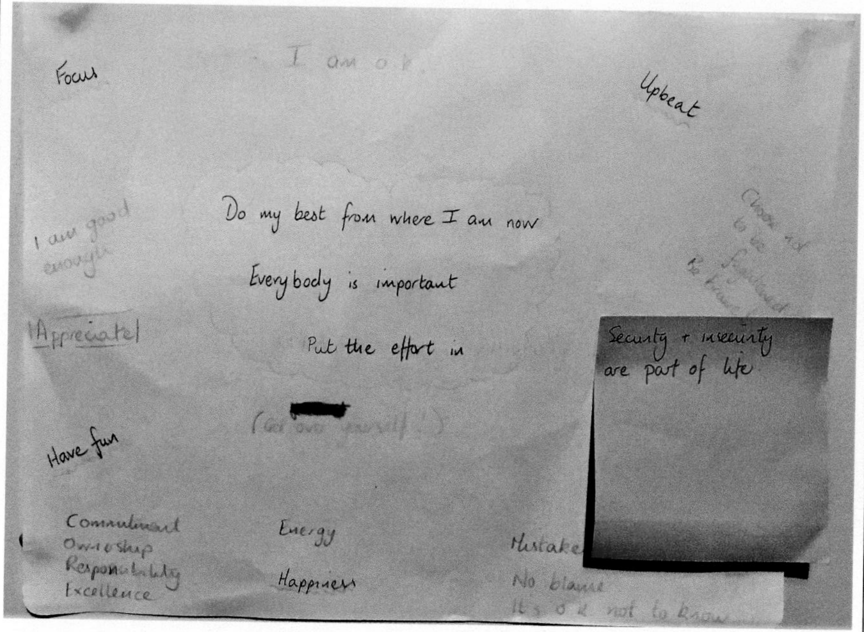

Focus	I am ok	Upbeat
I am good enough	Do my best from where I am now	Choose not to be frightened – be brave
Appreciate	Everybody is important	
	Put the effort in	Security and insecurity are part of life
Have fun	(Get over yourself)	
Commitment Ownership Responsibility Excellence	Energy Happiness	Mistakes No blame It is ok not to know

Figure 16.1 Kate's aide memoire (with transcript)

ethos that are expected in the delivery of the school's vision. It needs to speak to the future, with a positive, clear aspiration. Having a clear understanding of why certain core values resonate more than others through personal exploration is a helpful start.

All staff together

Whole staff process day 1: brainstorming

When I began the process of setting the vision for my school, I began by asking my colleagues to think about two key questions. The two questions were, on the face of it, very simple:

> **Question 1: What is important at our school?**
> **Question 2: What is unique about working here?**

My aim was that at the end of the process we would have considered, discussed and come to a shared understanding of what matters to us. This would lead to making explicit our values and then provide foundations for our vision statement.

I still have the post its notes and thoughts that arose from that day. What is interesting is that a lot of the potential challenges of management were dealt with through this process. It's a bit like the setting of class rules in September, colleagues through this process explored, discussed and without realising it began the process of agreeing, a set of operational guidelines. I have reproduced a selection of the responses in Fig. 16.2.

There are so many others, encompassing creativity, celebration, community and all this from two very simple questions. Obviously, this was not the end of the process. The next step was to group them into similar themes. This sharing and categorising bonded us as we explored common threads or differences. Following this we then discussed and agreed the overarching value that exemplified each set to a maximum of six. These would become the school's key values, acting as our agreed value base for adults' and children's behaviours.

Larger staff teams this can do this in groups, feeding back together at the end.

- Respecting differences of opinion
- Fair – people are treated fairly
- Individuality
- An environment where it doesn't matter if you get it wrong
- Welcoming environment
- Encourage children to be themselves, we are all unique
- Punctuality
- Professionalism
- Positive work ethic
- Learning about and portraying good morals
- Manners!
- High expectations (work and behaviour)
- Role modelling behaviour
- To persevere if things aren't going to plan
- Not being afraid of making mistakes
- Feeling comfortable to experiment and 'have a go'

Figure 16.2 Operational guidelines

Whole staff process day 2: the six themes in words and pictures

For the second day, I asked an educational psychologist and an artist/scriber to facilitate. As I said at the beginning of the chapter, we often have a mental image of a vision before we have the words. In this session we followed the HOPE approach ('Helping Our Pupils' Emotions': Mental Health Support for School Age Children and Their Families) whereby our discussion was translated into a visual image, with both words and pictures, as seen in Fig. 16.3.

This session resulted in a vibrant visual, containing all the key hopes and aspirations. These were not solely educational but also included colleagues hopes for themselves as part of a community. This wonderful, hopeful picture was displayed in our foyer for all to see. It embodied our vision for the school, for ourselves and for our community. We had our 'vision' and we had all created it. No one voice was more important in the process than another. It was then a simple step to put this into formal words. The most important part was that the words had been agreed by all, everyone

Figure 16.3 The finished result.

had an understanding of what this meant for us as adults, the expectations on us as a community of colleagues, of children and of families.

On reflection

I can honestly say that this process was a privilege. To sit alongside my colleagues and listen: to what deeply mattered to them, to the high standards they set for both themselves and our children, their commitment, their concern for families, their openness and honesty. It was a very humbling experience. Often on inset days like this it is tempting to think that we must have all the answers, that we must be seen to be 'delivering'. The success of this process, whatever activity you choose to use, relies on something far more difficult, which is sitting back and **truly listening**. This is one of the reasons it is beneficial to have fully considered your own values prior to exploring these questions within a team. When you have fully considered them, you are less likely to feel the need to force your views onto people. You can allow, facilitate and participate in an open discussion. You are secure in your thoughts, having given yourself the time to explore them fully beforehand.

We often ponder the difficulty of 'buy in' to a vision. Within this process, however, there is collaboration, and there will eventually be compromise, but the team has already 'bought in to it'. We have gone further: together we have created our safe, containing compassionate culture and all are committed to it

17

The role of the school leader

In this chapter, Kate describes the following features of school leadership:

1 *Ensuring teacher self-efficacy*
2 *Trust*
3 *Communication*
4 *Being a role model*
5 *Dealing with children 'sent' for misbehaviour*
6 *Community*
7 *Perspective and resilience*

It is through these elements, coupled with skilled leadership, that the school vision, the agreed values and teaching and learning frameworks are brought together. The details of these features demonstrate how to put the values into everyday life in a school so that they are authentically visible and tangible. Having the many strategies in place from the previous chapters for understanding and managing anxiety in all its forms, teachers and school leaders will now have a rich and powerful set of tools with which to create a wonderful, caring and compassionate, anxiety free school.

Teacher self-efficacy

Self-efficacy is our belief in our ability to achieve. A key aim in working with the staff of my school was to build their self-efficacy, and the process

DOI: 10.4324/9781003454434-22

of determining our vision and values contributed a great deal to the building of that belief. So much of what Shirley has written in Chapter 8 about self-efficacy applies not only to our children but directly to the staff who work with us. As with many things, there needs to be a mirrored staff culture: what we want for children we should also want for our colleagues.

Key factors

The challenge

Self-efficacy affects our approach to tasks in adulthood in the same way it does for pupils. We too have built a concept of ourselves (i.e., being capable and effective or not), based on our previous experiences. The challenge in school leadership is to keep the positive spark alive in our colleagues, accepting innovation whilst also delivering consistency and maintaining high standards. For leaders and a leadership team, tension exists between allowing exploration and ensuring that the core offer is effective, consistent and robust.

Believe in your staff

When I recruit staff, I am acutely aware that I need 'can do' people: staff who believe in their ability to effect change and who are keen to act and take responsibility. So, what leads to a team and individual members feeling effective? How can I create the optimum environment for personal responsibility? How can I enable staff to experience a deep sense of motivation and power? For me it's important that I convey *my* belief that they are effective, that they are capable, respected and valued amongst their peers. This resonates completely with the work Shirley has explored around pupils and their self-belief and the resulting pride that is experienced.

Co-constructing the success criteria: starting point for the criteria for any policy decision

I have found that, just as with pupils, if we co-construct our success criteria when looking at aspects of school life, teachers take this and run with it. If we return to the theme I mentioned when we looked at setting the vision in Chapter 16, this means thinking about the 'how' of being a leader and letting go of the 'who'. By this I mean really listening to others and letting go of the notion that as the school leader, everything I say is 'right'. It is important not to let my own sense of ego or power get in the way, as without really listening I become the equivalent of the adult helper who answers for the child, but in this case, I would be speaking for the staff.

It is difficult to stand back, because we still hold responsibility, but if we can let go of the fear that everything will fall apart, a much richer dialogue results. Yes, skilled facilitation is required through discussion, but as a leader our wisdom and experience can be used to pose questions and deepen consideration. I found the Education Endowment Fund's (EEF's) *Putting Evidence to Work: A School's Guide to Implementation* (2021) so helpful with this (see Fig. 17.1 and transcript). The checklist is up in my office and I refer to it when needed.

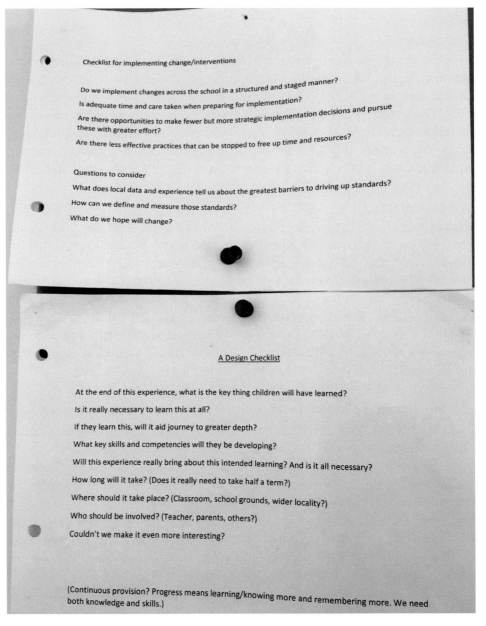

Figure 17.1 From the EEF's 'Putting Evidence to Work: A School's Guide to Implementation'.

Checklist for implementing change/intervention

Do we implement changes across the school in a structured and staged manner?

Is adequate time and care taken when preparing for implementation?

Are there opportunities to make fewer but more strategic implementation decisions and pursue these with greater effort?

Are there less effective practices that can be stopped to free up time and resources?

Questions to consider

What does local data and experience tell us about the greatest barriers to driving up standards?

What do we hope will change?

A Design Checklist

At the end of this experience, what is the key thing children will have learned?

Is it really necessary to learn this at all?

If they learn this, will it aid journey to greater depth?

What key skills and competencies will they be developing?

Will this experience really bring about this intended learning? And is it all necessary?

How long will it take? (Does it really need to take half a term?)

Where should it take place? (Classroom, school grounds, wider locality?)

Who should be involved? (Teacher, parents, others?)

Could we make it even more interesting?

(Continuous provision? Progress means learning/knowing more and remembering more. We need both knowledge and skills.)

Consultation in action
Discussion, listening and respect
The fact that I spend time listening does not mean that our discussions are a free for all. I usually begin with a key question. A 'How can we?' question (e.g., How can we improve, introduce, or alter a key aspect of school life?) I am sure as school leaders you have your own way of doing this, but I have found that allowing staff to fully discuss, without providing or pushing towards the answer that leadership wants to hear, is illuminating. Staff know that ultimately the decision rests with the Head, so this is their chance to influence and explain their classroom reality and for me to really hear their concerns and successes, interjecting and asking for clarification as the discussion unfolds. It is also important to hear all voices, as listening only to the loudest will skew a discussion. A reflection time needs to be built in for key changes, with the discussion being revisited two or three weeks later. Again, this allows colleagues to feel valued and listened to. Pitfalls and exciting, sometimes unexpected, successes can be shared. The life of the school has a heart driven by staff who know they are effective, and this is invaluable.

Valuing all voices and giving responsibility for objective decision making against the agreed criteria
What might at first seem like wishy washy 'listening' is in actuality highly crafted consultation. A question is posed, parameters explored and action agreed. This is revisited at an agreed date and time. Staff know at this point, refinement may be required, but that refinement is a direct result of their feedback and is again co constructed. The cycle is repeated but with a lengthier time between reviews. This approach works both with whole staff meetings and individually. The following anecdote describes one example of consultation in action.

Anecdote
A member of staff came to see me as she had heard about a new reading comprehension assessment scheme. The publicity around the scheme was such that she was convinced it would offer far more valuable information to staff on the gaps and the required interventions to close these. She was very keen to buy the scheme and introduce this to the whole school.

By listening to what she hoped to achieve through this change, I could sense the passion and drive to deliver the very best outcomes for pupils.

I was, however, happy that the current assessment delivered all we needed and that a change would be a great upheaval for staff. Further discussion revealed that the member of staff had read about this but did not know of anyone who was actually using the new scheme. At this point we both agreed that apart from the company's own PR we didn't have any real knowledge.

A further concern for me was the high cost of buying in a whole new school scheme.

By reaching for the 'Checklist for Implementing Change' we looked at the first point together. This moved the discussion from 'personal' to a more detached 'evidence based' one.

We discussed the fact that we had very little evidence to base a change on. The scheme could be amazing, or it could be a very costly mistake both financially and in staff time.

In order to implement change in a structured and staged manner, our first step would be to find out if it would be worth it.

My suggestion, therefore, was that the teacher would trial it alongside our existing scheme. She would then report back to me any benefits, differences or shortfalls in comparison with our usual assessment. I was happy to pay for one set of materials in order to facilitate this research and if the results were as striking as she believed we would switch.

This discussion meant that the teacher maintained her belief in her own ability. Furthermore, this was reinforced by the trust I put in her to research and report back, through a co- constructed plan. She maintained control, and would deliver the outcome to me, and because I knew that at the heart of it was the desire to do the best for the children, I trusted her to do a good job.

The very conditions that allow people to flourish (i.e., having the power to effect change, to have a sense of mastery and agency over our actions, to know people believe in our ability to try something out), are ones that we as leaders can find tricky to manage in staff. There are so many variables in schools that it can be hard to allow staff freedom when it comes to decision making. It can feel incredibly risky, especially when we know the scrutiny that comes with our job. Fear of standards and behaviour sliding rapidly downwards can make us grip ever tighter to the reins, with the unfortunate side effect that people can feel disenchanted and deskilled. Leaders are rightly keen to ensure consistency throughout the curriculum, within and across subjects and across year groups. The danger here though, is that this desire, whilst having a very laudable basis can, if we are not careful, lead to micromanagement, inflexibility and a 'because I say so' culture.

> **Follow up**
> *The staff member duly undertook both assessments with her class and arranged a time to report back to me. She was astounded when the new scheme did not offer anything radically different. She was delighted that she had trialled it before rolling it out to all staff and was relieved that there had not been an expensive unnecessary purchase. No, she informed me, we would not be buying it.*

The method of coming to this decision meant that the staff member concerned felt she truly owned the process and the decision. The sense of pride was tangible, and she knew I valued her voice. Had I vetoed this from the outset, the member of staff might well have become anxious about raising new possibilities for the school in the future. She might well have felt resentful and, ultimately, I would end up with a frustrated person. Through taking the time to meet, discuss and plan a way forward, her value as an effective member of staff was communicated to her.

In terms of self-efficacy, communication is so important. This sense of being valued and of having worth can be transmitted in very subtle ways. Staff, just like pupils, can pick up on differences, and these differences convey meaning, even if unintentionally.

Comparative rewards damage self – efficacy in all settings

In the school below, an unintended message was conveyed to staff about 'hard work' and 'worth'. This message had a direct impact on the teachers' sense of self, their sense of belonging and their desire to strive in the future. This anecdote parallels the giving of rewards (e.g., stickers or stars), mentioned in the previous section, to some children and not others for the same activity. The impact is the same whoever you are: a clear sense of how far you or your effort has been valued, leading to demoralisation and lowered self-efficacy for those who miss out. Even the teachers who received the bouquets in the following anecdote would have felt uncomfortable knowing that other teachers had not received the same.

> **Anecdote**
> *Staff in both Key Stage One (5–7 years old) and Key Stage Two (8–11 years old) were expected to stage separate performances annually. Both key stages worked hard on the productions. Those with the younger children introduced them to*

> *the idea of performing, some for the very first time. They built foundations, supported them with their lines, actions and dances ready for the big event.*
>
> *Staff with the older children used the foundations laid by their colleagues in previous years: they developed them and increased the sophistication of the acting in line with the age and stage of the children.*
>
> *At the end of the Key Stage One production, staff were thanked with a short speech and parents were encouraged to applaud. In contrast, at the end of the Key Stage Two production, staff were mentioned by name, they received individual bouquets of flowers in front of the parent audience and parents were encouraged to applaud many times.*

In terms of self-efficacy, the message was clear: Key Stage Two staff were perceived to have been more effective, to have worked harder, and therefore be worthy of greater praise than those in Key Stage One. The unintentional consequence of this generous action to one group of staff was to totally demoralise and disempower the other group.

Task not ego related praise: treat everyone the same

In terms of recognising and building self-efficacy, as far as is possible, I try to treat everyone the same: to pay attention to the unintended consequences of small acts. An example of this is that at Christmas or the end of a year, everyone gets exactly the same present. My teaching partners, office staff, cleaners, teachers and site manager all work equally hard and I'm genuinely thankful to all for the many essential roles well done.

This does not mean that individual praise is never given. I do say thank you and give praise where it's due. Just as with pupils, however, I try to be specific about what the thanks and praise is for. As with children, ego related praise is counterproductive. The thanks, therefore, must be specific to a task or particular piece of work that has been carried out with diligence. This praising of the behaviour reinforces my high expectations; it shows that I notice the effort and the care. It also helps with feedback when someone is struggling, as the language of school is about the work rather than a person being a 'good' or 'bad' teacher. Within the staff team this reduces anxiety and I have found that it creates an atmosphere where people 'notice' and appreciate the acts of others. The team often seek out those they know to have a special skill in a particular area. Recognition is shared and everyone has a chance to shine. Our role as school leaders, with ultimate responsibility, is to inspire our team and provide the conditions for staff to shine.

As Benjamin Zander (2011) says, of his role as a leader: 'Who am I being, that their eyes aren't shining?

Trust

Leadership is more than management

For me trust is the lynchpin of so much that we achieve as a school team. I trust my staff to behave professionally, I respect their opinions, I trust that we are all working towards the same goal, but how do I convey that trust to them?

Conveying trust is a powerful tool

I have to hold myself to the same professional standards I expect of them and their dealings with parents, professionals and each other. I know how tempting it can be to snap, to eye roll after a conversation, but if I do, what message am I conveying and what permissions am I giving for that to become the norm in our communications with one another? How anxious will staff feel if they cannot believe that what I say is what I mean? How trustworthy do I seem if my words and actions differ?

Creating clear expectations reduces anxiety

Similarly, if I say I trust my staff but then go on to micromanage every situation, staff will soon feel stifled and anxious at the scrutiny that comes with this. It is hard to let go of control, but if clear guidelines are in place about how and when information will be communicated to me and from me, how key decisions are reached against agreed criteria, then there is freedom and security. It is important to me that staff know that their expertise matters; that they experience themselves as equal partners.

My emphasis on listening is in order to create an environment where it is not about 'winning' a conversation, or coming out as 'top dog', but about the shared desire to do the best for our children.

Communication

Every interaction conveys a message

As we know the school day is packed full of communications: greeting children, parents and staff, problem solving, teaching, guiding, working with multi agency professionals, safeguarding, health and safety and so on. It is impossible to count up how many interactions there are within a school day. Sometimes it can feel as though the conversations that are needed get in the way of the 'real' job. How many times do we stop and think 'I haven't achieved anything today?' and yet when we look back over the last hours, we have been constantly in conversation on work-related matters just maybe not the ones on our 'to-do' list?

There is so much information available about positive communication skills (i.e., open questions, active listening, checking and rephrasing), all of which are hugely beneficial. Alongside those skills, and those outlined in the previous chapter, I have developed some very simple strategies that I find support open and mutually respectful dialogue.

Approaching empathy sideways

This strategy is one I use when I'm finding it hard to empathise. Most of us are familiar with and understand empathy. It is a very powerful tool. It is the idea that you truly 'put yourself in the shoes' of another person, see the situation from their perspective, including all the complexities that they face. This has the power to open up dialogue in a supportive and equal way rather than eliciting pity. Sometimes when I'm struggling with this, I reframe the situation and ask myself 'how would I like my adult child to be treated in this situation?' I have found this to be an exceptionally helpful thought as it accesses empathy, but sideways.

Anecdote

Many years back I worked with a teacher who whilst wanting to do the best for the children, found it difficult to juggle all the many parts required. This resulted in a negative impact on children's learning and much unhappiness all round.

I was required to speak with the teacher and put in place a formal support plan. At first, I struggled to be empathetic, as this person had massively increased my workload. Then a thought popped into my head 'If this was my adult child in front of me, what would I want for them?'

For my own child I would want clarity, honesty and realism. I would not want irritation or blame. It lessened both the staff member's anxiety and my own and brought warmth to some difficult conversations. It became far easier to communicate, to find a compassionate way forward, to deliver honest feedback reflecting the situation accurately, and paved the way for change.

This simple reframe transformed my meetings. It didn't change the issues to be dealt with but helped me to see a way forward. This must be differentiated from rescuing. Just as the job of a parent is at times to scaffold support that allows the child to grow and develop, so it is for us as leaders. I now use this mental trick when I am on the edge of irritation with a person, be they a colleague or a parent.

Avoiding avoidance

Next is a phrase I use when faced with a difficult situation; it helps me to see the benefit of dealing with something head on.

> **Anecdote**
> *My then teenage son was trying to find a way of telling his girlfriend that he no longer wanted to go out with her. He had tied himself in knots trying to find a way to deliver an unhappy message happily and as a result had delayed telling her. He came to the conclusion that 'you can't turn bad news into good'.*

I now use this phrase myself when something uncomfortable needs addressing. It is remarkably effective as it highlights that the situation will not change however long it is left, and it definitely won't disappear. Avoidance may feel good in the short term but ultimately heightens anxiety for all. Far better, therefore, to face the difficulty, deal with it and move on.

A checklist for communication

Lastly, just like my checklist for change, I have a checklist for communication. This consists of four questions and has been adapted from Steve Peters (2012)

• Is now a good time for this conversation?	We all know the frustration that can come from being interrupted when we are in the middle of something. The school day has peaks and troughs all its own. It pays dividends to be mindful of these and where possible choose a time wisely. This may seem blindingly obvious, but when we're intent on crossing an item off our to-do list, we may be causing stress and anxiety for someone else. Pausing and checking 'Is now a good time for you?' literally takes a minute. It shows respect and that the issue to be addressed requires attention. If it's not the best time, schedule one that is and keep to it.

• Is this the right place?	How tempting to 'catch' someone in the corridor. For some queries this is fine but not all.
• Am I clear what I need?	If I'm not clear, then I may well be asking the wrong question. It is worth spending time focusing on the desired outcome so that any questions relate to a) directly achieving the outcome and b) uncovering any likely difficulties or hindrances. Agreed actions will then be less likely to overcomplicate things or take staff off course.
• What is the 'particularness' of the person I am about to speak with?	We spend much time thinking about our pupils, making small adjustments in our interactions in order to get the best out of them. I do this with staff as well.

This checklist has saved me a great deal of time and stress over the years, and I expect it has done the same for the staff I speak with too.

Being a role model

How I manage myself in the many interactions I have throughout the day is vitally important. As teachers we are all role models. However, this can sometimes be misinterpreted as having to be perfect.

Role modelling and perfection are not the same thing

Somewhere along the way, we have lost the idea that as working professionals, mistakes are ok. This puts a huge burden on us and heightens anxiety unnecessarily. Successful people make mistakes, let's not add shame to our day. We need to own our mistakes, put them right and move on. We also need to allow our colleagues to make honest mistakes too.

> **Anecdote**
>
> *I remember a conversation I had with a senior colleague many years ago, when I first held a leadership position. It was literally one of my first days, and I said how nervous I was of making a mistake. My colleague incredibly sharply retorted that their role was 'to make sure I didn't make any mistakes'. I remember instantly my anxiety shot through the roof. I was new in role and now it was made very clear that mistakes in any shape or form were not to be tolerated.*

Mistakes are normal: it's how we respond to them that matters

This experience, although hair – raising for me at the time, helped me to make a very useful distinction, one that I state explicitly to staff now: mistakes are o.k. but sloppiness isn't. In order for staff to believe that I mean this, I have to apologise when I've forgotten to do something, missed something or simply got in a muddle. It's not always comfortable, but it does create an environment where we're kinder to each other. It paves the way for openness and significantly reduces worry and fear. I also need to respond supportively when someone 'owns up' to a mistake and together find a way to sort it out. It takes great courage to own up to your boss and I am grateful that my staff trust me enough to do this.

Anecdote

I had been out of the school building and on my return one of my teachers came to see me and said they had to tell me of something that they had done wrong. She had been using the cooking area and had put a hot induction pan on the work surface, leaving an unsightly stain. She was very sorry especially as the work top was new. I thanked her for telling me and checked that health and safety procedures with the children had been followed, which they had. I reassured her that everything was fine, that she wouldn't be the last person to mark the work top, it was just uncomfortable being the first. The staff member looked incredibly relieved and we talked about how the lesson had gone.

How brave was the staff member, to willingly come and own up? Without an open culture, I could have been left wondering who had done this and what else didn't I know about? Through such honesty, however, I was completely in the picture. It was a genuine mistake, the children were safe, so did it really matter? No. It was disappointing, but better that the area is used for the education of the children than left to become a show kitchen through fear of leaving a mark.

Leadership is more than management

I feel very strongly that I have a responsibility to set the tone in the school. If I think about people I like spending time with, it is often those who bring good cheer, are warm hearted, with a lightness of being. They create an environment that is comfortable and uplifting, where it's ok to be yourself. I want this for my pupils, families and staff. I therefore have to create this through my interactions. This is not about creating a false jollity, but approaching people with warmth and an upbeat attitude. As part of this it is also important to acknowledge and attribute hard work and effort so that people know their contribution matters. I have found when I do this people respond in kind, creating a mutually supportive working environment.

Students sent for misbehaviour

Part of our role as teachers is to develop pupils and prepare them for adulthood. When a child makes a mistake within their academic learning, we are skilled at addressing it, unpacking the misconception and re-teaching through the provision of examples and practice, until the child grasps the concept. This is usually done in a very calm and systematic way. I find this approach also works well when children are struggling with their behaviour. Misbehaviour reveals a gap in learning, and I have found shouting or presenting as extremely cross in this situation counterproductive. The child will feel under threat and as a result may resort to a fight, flight or freeze response (e.g., escalation through engaging in defiant, argumentative behaviour, an attempt to get out of the situation or shut down). Anxiety levels escalate and the stress hormone cortisol will have a field day in both the child and the adult. This shuts down the child's capacity to take in or process information. The opportunity to learn from the mistake has passed.

Misbehaviour creates an opportunity for learning

By approaching misbehaviour as a gap in learning, an opportunity appears. The school values (respect, responsibility etc.) are very helpful here and are the gateway into a calm discussion about why the behaviour is unacceptable, what needs to take place to make amends and why. The discussion is around unacceptable behaviour rather than being an unacceptable child. I hope that by following this model the children in school are given the opportunity to build secure, trusting attachments that will serve them well as blueprints in later life.

The following transcript is of a conversation I had with an 8 year old child (R) sent to me for misbehaviour. Angela has provided her analysis of the strategies I used.

The conversation	Angela's analysis
The child that had been sent to me arrived in my office crying.	*Kate would have immediately acknowledged and managed her own emotions the second she saw R arriving in her office upset and crying. This scene might have triggered a whole range of memories and emotions for Kate. She might have felt like scooping R up and reassuring her. She might have felt angry if she had time pressures that day. She would have acknowledged these thoughts, reactions and emotions in a matter of seconds, almost unconsciously, and then consciously modelled a calm and containing School Leader for R.*
KM Come on in sweetheart, I can see already that you wish you hadn't done whatever it is that you're here to talk about, alright. So, tell me what's happened? Do you need a tissue? *The child nods and I pass her the tissues.*	*Kate reduces R's shame before even beginning to ask her to think about what she has done. She just acknowledges R's distress. Kate names R's upset feelings and calls her 'sweetheart' (i.e., you're still loveable). Kate provides a tissue.*
KM So tell me what's happened sunshine? **R** I was just talking in class	*Kate calls R sunshine as she ascertains what happened, bringing a light touch, conveying the message that seeing the School Leader is not as scary as she might have been imagining. She reduces fear and anxiety.*
KM You were talking in class, ok, and then what happened? Was it a time when you were meant to be talking? *The child shook her head.* **R** No. **KM** No. *(In a very quiet voice)* Dry those eyes. Was that it? Because you must've been doing that a lot for you to be here, mustn't you? So tell me, do you think it was or do you feel it wasn't?' **R** Um, it was a lot.	*Kate whispers, 'Dry those eyes' as R's acknowledgement that she shouldn't have been talking makes her cry more. Kate speaks very quietly as she addresses the fact that R must have been talking a lot. The quiet voice promotes closeness and trust and reduces the shame and anxiety, so that R can admit she spoke a lot.*

The conversation	Angela's analysis
KM It was a lot. Thank you for being honest – that's really, really important. That takes courage and you've shown one of our values, and when we spoke last week, I was really proud of you for telling the truth and you've done the same again today. So, what should you have been doing?' **R** Um, maths. **KM** Ok, and can you hold what you were talking about for playtime? And talk about it at playtime? *The child nods* **KM** Yes, ok. So, what would make it better do you think? **R** Um, just saying things at playtime. **KM** Just saying things at playtime, definitely. And can you have a look at our values? *Child turns and looks at the value display in my room.* **KM** Which ones were you not showing? **R** Respect? **KM** Yes, definitely not showing respect. So what could you do now? **R** Not talk. **KM** Yes, anything else that might make it a bit better? *There's a pause as the child thinks.* **R** Don't say stuff, just say it at playtime. *Another pause*	*Kate says, 'Thank you for being honest … that takes courage … I'm proud of you', building R's self-esteem. Then Kate can begin to help R to think about solutions, such as holding back conversations until playtime.* *Kate and R can then think together, looking at the values display. R considers that she was not showing respect. Kate agrees with this, then slowly and gently helps R to also think about responsibility, leading to R realising she could apologise. Further joint thinking takes place. R suggests she apologise to the teaching partner and the class teacher. Kate suggests she also apologises to her friend, who would have been distracted from her maths. Many pauses take place in this interaction, allowing the pre-frontal cortex, the thinking brain, to work, to not be overcome with emotions.*

The conversation	Angela's analysis
KM Yes, what else do we often do if we've upset somebody, or we've not taken responsibility?	
R Say sorry?	
KM *nodding* Mmm, Is that something you feel you could do?	
Child nods	
KM Ok. Who do you need to say sorry to?	
The child names the teaching partner and the class teacher.	
KM And who else?	
There is another pause.	
KM What about the person you were talking to?	
The child says her friend's name.	
KM Ok, what was she trying to do? Was she trying to do her maths while you were talking?	
Another long pause, then the child nods.	
KM Yes, she was. So, can you see, by not taking responsibility for your own learning, you were actually disturbing somebody else, so it's not always that you're talking, it's that you're stopping someone else from doing what they're trying to do. Can you see that?	
The child nods.	
KM Yes, is there anything else I need to know? Anything that you haven't told me or that Mrs K hasn't told me?	
The child shakes her head.	
R No.	

The conversation	Angela's analysis
KM So that was it? *The child nods* **KM** Ok, So, do you need me to come with you to say sorry? *She shakes her head.* **KM** No. So you can manage that on your own? And I'll check, ok?' *She nods.* **KM** So what do I need to see this afternoon? **R** Um, not talking. **KM** What else? What might I check that you've been doing? **R** Getting on with my work? **KM** Getting on with your work. So if we have a little chat at the end of the day will you be able to show me and tell me that you've done some really hard work? **R** *(nods and whispers)* Yes. **KM** I'm really proud of you for showing courage and telling the truth, because I know you find that difficult, so I'm really proud of you.	*When Kate ask R if she needs her to come with her to say sorry, R shakes her head. Kate accepts R's decision but says she will check on her. This is not only a way of ensuring the proper apologies are made but is also a really important way of letting R know that she is being kept in mind. Kate is thinking about her and will take time to see her at the end of the day. The message is that Kate cares about R and wants her to work hard and do well at school.* *The conversation ends with a reinforcement of Kate being proud of R, of her courage and her honesty. R will leave Kate's office knowing that Kate cares about her, is thinking about her, is proud of her, sees her as strong and courageous and wants the best for her. Within this context, R will be able to take in the lesson that she must talk less in class. Once shame is lessened, children can think about how to make changes. Maslow – when you feel safe and loved and valued, you can access your cognitive brain and find solutions.* *Finally, Kate will take some time that day or evening to process her emotions around this encounter. If she listens to herself, she will know which emotions she needs to work on and resolve, thus looking after her own emotional health.*

This is just one example. It really is a dialogue and is used as a way of explaining and supporting mistakes. There are times when a discussion will need to involve other children together, or even staff and children. My way of explaining to the child is that something must have happened to make the teacher think that/see that/etc. And it's also important if that hasn't happened that we can sort out the misunderstanding, with care and sensitivity.

Enabling a child to understand and make amends is of vital importance. It lessens shame, as Angela explains, and builds trust whilst also giving a strong message that the child has the skills and is able to sort it out (self-efficacy).

Trust and respect are an important part of making amends

The building of trust is important. Children feel safe and contained when they know they will be listened to, when they trust that they will be treated fairly. They are better able to take responsibility for their part in a disagreement, to own it and move on if they are not holding on to resentment that someone else has 'got away with it'. It is commonplace to explore and kindly challenge children on inconsistencies within a re-telling, in order to find out the facts.

This exploration can be difficult if a child is adamant that the situation has been incorrectly reported by an adult. When this occurs, it is important to involve the adult in respectful exploration of the event with the child.

The adult must not be undermined in this process. In order to guard against this, I begin by saying that I know the staff member tells the truth, so there must be a misunderstanding, a missing piece of the jigsaw or something that has not yet been said. I also say that the adult really wouldn't want to get this wrong or to have told the child off for no reason – that it's important to them as well. At this point I say to the member of staff 'isn't that right?' to which they always agree. This leaves the conversation open for the adult and the child. It becomes a joint process and together we can work it out. We then go step by step through what the child says and what the adult saw. This joint exploration conveys to the child that they matter, the tone in which the conversation is carried out shows that crucially the adult is an ally, ensuring that we have all the information and that they too, do not want a child to be in trouble unfairly. This does not excuse the child, but it gives an important message that we are all working together. Again, our school values are used, we talk about the courage it takes to tell the truth, how respect is important especially when you disagree with someone, how it takes courage to apologise if you have got something wrong etc. In my experience, if the adult has missed a vital piece of information, the original action that they witnessed remains. It then becomes a case of addressing the additional information. The adult often feels for the child and is genuinely concerned for them 'If you'd told me that before I could have sorted it out, we wouldn't have had to come to Mrs Moss'. This joint problem-solving models to the child that differences can be resolved; it gives a blueprint for this if they find themselves in a pickle again.

It is important to me that my staff know I will explore any issues thoroughly. This gives them permission to do the same. Sometimes this exploration takes time and staff need to know that they are allowed to take as much care unpicking disagreements and supporting the children to make amends as necessary. They also need to know that if I join them in this, my starting point is that they are trusted professionals, that I am not doubting what they saw but helping a young child to navigate the necessity of telling the adults around them the whole truth, in order to deal with a situation fairly.

Restorative practice

Restorative practice is built on foundations of positive relationships: respect, responsibility, the need to repair any damage caused and the willingness of the community to allow reintegration. Through this, children know that any matter will be looked into in full and that there is an expectation that all people, both adults and children, will take responsibility for their actions. Through restorative practice, children are helped to understand the impact of their actions on others and are given support to make amends and 'restore' the relationship, repairing harm through respectful conversation and reintegration. This process is important as it builds self-efficacy, especially for the impulsive child. It develops the idea that the child has some control, is required to take responsibility and that their actions have consequences. When it is skilfully implemented its power can move a child from a reactive external locus of control (i.e., 'they made me do it') to an internal one with the development of understanding, agency and empathy.

Community

In our job we often talk of 'key stakeholders'. This term belies the many and varied people that make up the complexity of our community. We consist of so many different parts, we have parents, extended families, the local town, village or parish in which the school is located, staff, governors, the parent teacher association, and for some, church membership too. It is therefore reasonable to expect that we won't all agree all the time. In our job we see the very best of people and occasionally the very worst. When things are going well, and everyone pulls in the same direction, it genuinely is a wonderful community to be part of. I have found a few things help to promote this feeling and can be useful when it doesn't feel quite so wonderful. They are quite simple, and I expect most school leaders are already naturally doing them:

Be visible. It's so much easier to begin conversations and find out what parents really think when you're out and about.

Use inclusive language in letters and official communications as this tends to promote togetherness. For example, we are delighted that our children …

Bear the emotion. When someone is upset or frustrated allow them to be so. We know that we need to do this with children when they are upset, anxious or angry in order to get to a point where we can talk productively, however, it is also important to do this with adults. Allow people to let off steam without interrupting or correcting, just listen and clarify the main points the person brings. It's so tempting to try to shut a conversation down, particularly an angry parent, in an effort to make the problem go away. If you immediately respond with a counter argument, however, the person will feel that you are not listening, that you haven't appreciated how much the issue is a concern and it will catapult you into opposing corners. Experience has shown me that people tend to have a natural time limit when expressing very strong emotions, which is around 10 minutes. After this time, they will be far more receptive to a rational discussion of the problem. The emotion will have dissipated somewhat, leaving space for exploration. Rather than finding yourself fighting with the person, you can work together to find a solution. Just knowing that the outburst will not go on for ever is hugely helpful and lessens the stress response in ourselves.

Try not to judge. Just as children who are grouped by ability know exactly what the teacher thinks of their intelligence, so parents can tell if teachers and office staff are judging them. This is the opposite of feeling included within a community and, at its extreme, sets up an 'us and them' situation. Don't assume that your staff will see or appreciate the complexities of different families' lives, as we know we can only see the world through the experiences that we have been through. Sometimes it is helpful to ask a staff member who is struggling with a particular parent to step into their shoes so that they can truly see and feel the parent's world.

Anecdote

Office staff found one particular parent very difficult to deal with. The parent was hard to get hold of when the child was absent. Because of their frustration, any conversations tended to be terse. Whilst the words used by the office staff were inoffensive, the tone in which the query about the reason for absence was asked, left no doubt that this individual was seen as a 'bad' parent.

I spoke with staff and explained that the child had issues separating from the parent. This stemmed from early childhood trauma; in particular, violence within the home. Initially staff expressed the opinion that the person was just rude and awkward. We then discussed further how you might view the world if you have been viciously attacked. We talked about how difficult it would be to trust, the discussion was wide ranging and showed a deep compassion within the team.

Just this additional knowledge changed staff's approach: they moved from judgement to genuine concern. Slowly, over time, the parent began to ring in themselves, and I would often hear the staff member ask if there was anything they could do to help.

Empathy is easy when we agree with the person but much harder when we don't, and yet this is the time when it is most needed. Once the staff member appreciated the parent's difficulties and what they had been through, the tension within the interactions changed, their communications contained less judgement and the parent on the receiving end felt that they mattered within the community.

Perspective and resilience

The educational landscape and what we are responsible for changes often and the fear of missing a vital change from the Department for

Education in England (DfE) or any national policy holders, can present a challenge to our overall wellbeing. Within the school day we are responsible for managing not only the education of our pupils but also, increasingly, to support the emotional, financial and occasionally marital difficulties of the families we work with. It is a real privilege that people trust us with exceptionally sensitive personal information, but it can also feel, at times, overwhelming. This lack of control over what we might be presented with daily, can change our outlook and wear us down. As one local school leader said to me recently, *'I live in fear'*. This is such a sad yet honest reflection of what many educational professionals feel.

Acceptance of our limits leads to better emotional health

So, what can help to alleviate this and keep our sense of tasks and what is expected of us in perspective? Again, we come back to the 'how' of leadership: it is how I deal with things (i.e. in line with my values), that matters. If I focus on creating an environment where the conditions for learning, growth, development and support are in place to the best of my ability, with the resources I have at hand, I cannot do more. These conditions, all layered together, increase the chances of educational success and emotional stability for my pupils and staff. I cannot control what happens for each person beyond this. I find this viewpoint helps me to keep perspective and, because I believe in the power of the environment that my team and I create, I have the resilience to continue.

For me this is where our values really do help. If we can accept that the sands shift often in education and judge our behaviour against our values and consequent actions, rather than outcomes, we will see that in the main we are doing a very good job. Once we have acknowledged this, it is easier to positively face another day.

Last words

It is worth, at this point, reviewing the conditions for a contained, compassionate classroom and school which is the ultimate aim of everything you have read so far. In Chapter 2, linked with projection and containment, these were placed to give an overview of what was to come. Reproduced here, they form a summary of everything written so far.

Conditions for a classroom culture of containment

- **Create a structured and predictable routine** in the classroom
- **Make the classroom safe**, with no potential 'weapons'
- Create a **calm** corner in the classroom
- Speak **quietly, calmly and lovingly**
- Encourage children to **share worries** with teacher and friends – worry/chat box
- Create a culture of talking in the classroom where children can **share emotions, opinions and worries**
- Give a message that **all emotions are valuable and** acceptable – name different kinds of emotions so they are understood whenever the opportunity arises

Conditions for a whole school culture of containment

- **Trust** and **openness** between all staff
- **Open doors**
- Being **available** for parents wherever possible
- Schools are **communities**: encouraging active parental involvement
- Being creative with **break times**
- Considering children who are overwhelmed in **large gatherings**
- **Connecting** with children and with each other
- **Modelling happiness: smiles** trigger hormonal changes helping neurons connect
- Being **genuine** and **interested** in the child and colleagues – even when hard
- **Listening** attentively
- **Thanking** children for sharing with you
- Having positive **body language**
- Being **consistent**

Positive school experiences build resilience

18

Looking after yourself

In this crucial final chapter, Angela first discusses the importance of managing the rigour of school life while still protecting your own mental health. Kate's experiences and strategies then follow.

Can I work on containing myself?

The simple answer is yes. We are all responsible for containing ourselves. It is called looking after yourself. If we look back to Part I on projection and containment, we'll remember the attentive, listening, calming adult in the face of projections: the containing adult. But what does that adult need to do to increase their capacity to contain? They need to know themselves and to look after themselves.

Knowing myself

We generally manage to look after our physical health, such as attending health appointments, exercising and so on. Many of us are also pretty good at looking after ourselves socially. We are less good at turning to our emotional health. It can make us feel very vulnerable to admit to feeling sad, mad or bad: we'd all sooner be the strong ones. Yet this approach can be detrimental to our emotional wellbeing. How many times have you called

DOI: 10.4324/9781003454434-23

yourself an idiot for forgetting something, for buying the wrong item, for being short with someone? What would your best friend say if you told them? They would be more empathic than you are. They would say 'everyone forgets, everyone makes mistakes'. They'd be there for you, on your side. We need to be on our own sides more, which means knowing ourselves, with all our strong points and our vulnerabilities.

The children need you to know yourself so you can help them to know themselves

Anecdote

I was working as a SENDCo in a busy town school with an experienced School Leader called Margaret. She was excellent with the school community, very supportive of staff and made sure she knew every child and their families.

As a SENDCo, a particular boy, Aaron, was well known to me. He had a troubled home life with a father in and out of prison. I was working in my room one morning when Margaret came in with a panicked look on her face. In an unusually distressed voice, she asked me to come urgently to her room. I followed her and as we went down the stairs through the school, she explained that Aaron had locked himself in her cupboard.

I had previously worked in residential units for children and had experience of this kind of behaviour. I also felt Margaret's panic and instinctively became very calm. I had no thoughts as I walked through the door of her room. She called through the door. 'Aaron, Mrs Evans is here now to speak to you'. I felt the pressure on me to sort this out. I spoke quietly through the door – 'Hello Aaron. How you doing in there?' No reply. Margaret looked at me with exasperation. I could imagine what was going through her head – safeguarding, health and safety, the parents, calling the police to get him out, the embarrassment.

After a few more attempts to communicate with Aaron, I sat down outside the door and started chatting out loud to myself. 'Gosh, this carpet is softer than I had thought'. 'It's quite comfy and safe here'. I was aware of trying to promote a sense of safety in Margaret and in Aaron. I was also aware that I was shooting in the dark, just chatting randomly and staying calm. Not panicking seemed to be the most important thing I could do.

Margaret had by now sat down on her chair and was visibly relaxing as she handed over to me, projecting her power into me. I in turn felt pretty powerless inside but knew I couldn't show it. Eventually Aaron began to answer me. We chatted some more. When the time felt right, I asked him if he'd like to have a walk with me. He unlocked the door from the inside and walked out. We went for a short walk. Margaret stayed in her room. With his agreement, I returned Aaron to his class teacher, who welcomed him back.

I had managed to model calm while feeling unsure of the outcome. It had been such an unknown outcome. With children who are not governed by their thinking in that moment, adults need to be prepared for any eventuality. We had to sit with our uncertainty. This uncertainty and powerlessness, of course, was exactly what Aaron was feeling. He had successfully projected it into us. And had projected his terror into Margaret.

Educators need to know themselves and to recognise and manage their emotions in order to help children who are overwhelmed by their emotions and who can't find a way out.

You're important

Here's a list just for educators in schools, to help you in your endeavour of looking after yourselves. **You're important and you deserve to look after yourselves**. Not all of it might be manageable but getting some 'me' time is your responsibility. It needn't take long. Just think of one thing you'd like to do this week to look after yourself. Make sure you do it, and then do it again. Working on looking after yourself is easy work once you get used to it and it becomes part of your life.

Conditions for staff care
• Support from senior management • Support and understanding from colleagues • More resources • Me time • Family time • Less 'paper' work • Courses on how to look after myself • Appreciation • Permission to get things wrong /discuss them openly without worry about being seen as not good at my job • Encouragement and recognition

Kate now describes typical experiences of a teacher and a school leader, and how self-care and self-management are critical to being able to not only function, but also to feel a sense of control and therefore enjoyment out of the demands of working in education.

A log of my morning from 7.55 am to 8.15 am

Anecdote

7.55

I arrive in the school car park. The Chair of the P.T.A. is waiting for me and stands by my car as I get out. She apologises for pouncing on me but explains she wants to talk through the arrangements for the upcoming Easter event, in particular what happens if it rains? So, we discuss this and agree on the back-up plan.

Whilst this conversation takes place a child runs over to me waving an absence form.

I speak with the parent of the child, reminding them of the importance of school attendance and explaining why I will not be authorising the absence in this case.

I walk into the school foyer to discover a caterpillar on the rug. As I look closer, I see a few more and realise, to my horror, that they are either maggots or moth larvae. I find a tissue, pick them up and put them in the bin. Our caretaker is called to come and deal with the problem, which he does immediately.

I walk along the corridor heading to my office, a staff member follows me and informs me about a communication she had received from a parent. The communication implies that the parent wants something from home stuck up on the classroom wall. We discuss how she will sensitively deal with this, as well as check that the parent is ok.

The SENDCo arrives and stands next to the teacher, waiting for us to finish talking, then she updates me on some communications with a paediatrician and other outside agencies in relation to a particular child.

My phone pings and a member of staff informs me they have a very upset stomach and won't be in today, I'm grateful she won't be sharing her bug, but now need to find someone able to work 1–1 with a child.

A Stem Ambassador arrives to deliver workshops to the children. I show him to the hall.

Another teacher comes into the corridor to use the photocopier, and I take the opportunity to check she's received my email about a new starter beginning on Monday with no spoken English. She has and is prepared.

I walk into my office, put down my bag and take off my coat.

It is only 8.15 am.

Full on, wonderful but intense!

This is typical of the start everyone working in a school has, but especially school leaders. It's full on, and wonderful, when you have the energy to deal with it. When we are tired, however, or if we are not looking after ourselves, these important impromptu conversations and events can feel a little trapping. They can cause anxiety as the demand and pressure to provide answers and deal immediately with situations grows. This is especially true if you like time to reflect and think things through before deciding on a course of action.

When we are in school, the pace is absolutely non-stop. Whether you are classroom based or your leadership role is outside of the classroom, your feet will not touch the ground once your school day begins. This is why it is so important to balance the intensity of the school day with good mental health.

I was very fortunate that my very first head teacher, a wonderful man, had a very full and busy life outside of school. He would come in on a Monday with tales of his amateur dramatic society, his church and his family. He expected us to have full lives too. This early modelling showed that there was life to be lived beyond the school gate and was invaluable to me.

The need for control

We all have pastimes and needs that bring us pleasure. Peters (2012) speaks of our basic emotional needs and drives that give us the impetus to get up and do something, for example, socialising, enjoying food, curiosity, a need for power, a need for security, and so on. Different ones will resonate for different people and the individual feels pleasure when these needs are met. When life is smooth, we manage these easily, but when times become more difficult the balance may become off kilter. A common one for teachers is a need for control.

Anecdote

As a young student, I remember sitting down in a staff room. There was an audible gasp and I was ushered into another chair by kindly colleagues. I was quite bewildered, but over the next few weeks came to understand that one member of staff viewed that particular chair as her own and would refuse to sit in any other spot. The domain around the chair was also hers and woe betide anyone that challenged this.

> *This caused stress for everybody, the unfortunate person who accidently sat in the chair and the member of staff who spent her time angrily defending it from perceived trespassers.*

This desire for control is a great asset most of the time as it means people are happy to take responsibility for tasks and decisions in their day to day lives, but we have all experienced a situation where someone has taken this need for control to an extreme. When we are over tired, we can tighten our grip, causing further stress, or do the complete opposite and loosen it far too much, again causing ourselves distress.

How many times have you decided that you will not eat whatever treat is in the staffroom today but somehow found yourself tucking in? Then you've berated yourself with all sorts of harsh criticism? You might have built a store of secret resources, such as glue sticks or rulers that are meant for sharing, or you might have worked with a colleague who did this. Other examples are the holding on to a piece of information, such as a change to routine, that could have been helpful to share, over-sharing, or withholding alongside unrealistic expectations of others.

This tightening and loosening of control causes stress not only to ourselves, but also to those around us. As we lose our own perspective, we often expect those around us to be mind-readers and to 'know' that we want a job carried out in a certain way, or that something should have been left well alone. We might then blame the other person and be blind to our own contribution to the situation. The resulting irritations, upset and a feeling that those around you are 'walking on eggshells' creates an unhealthy and unhappy dynamic for all involved. If we know our own patterns and responses to the build-up of stress, we can put in reminders and alerts (as we would for the children in our care) to take a moment to add in whatever healthy action is restorative and see this as a necessary part of our lives.

Not looking after ourselves can have serious consequences

The more tired or stressed we become the more difficult it is to hold a sense of perspective and manage these needs.

So many people that I speak with feel guilty if they're not working, as there is always so much to do. They lose the 'fun' elements of their lives or approach leisure activities with a desperation that makes them seem like a yet another chore. This means that there is a very real risk of burnout. It is, therefore, of vital importance that we pay attention to ourselves and our emotional barometer, and make sure our basic emotional needs and drives are safely met.

If we don't, we can so easily become ground down. I think of it like a battery draining that requires recharging regularly. The difficulty, of course, is that the more tired and stressed we become, the harder the recharge can be, which impacts our enjoyment of all areas of life. Alongside this, feeling stress and anxiety is often accompanied by a highly critical internal commentary outlining all the ways in which we are 'failing,' both within and outside of work.

A self-care strategy

If we are drained for an exceptionally long time, we can also lose touch with the things that bring us joy, but there is a brilliant self-care tool that can help: Fig. 18.1.

We all like and need different things, whether this is time alone, with friends, with family, or something else entirely. Attending to our own emotional needs means we will be more able to support the many needs of our pupils. This self-care tool helps individuals to identify what's missing and see ways of putting the joy back into life. I highly recommend investing some time looking at this and then taking steps to ensure that you are looking after yourself.

Using PETI

The PETI model (see Fig. 18.2) that Shirley describes to develop children's meta-cognition and self-efficacy when they come up against a problem can also be applied to ourselves and our emotional health.

It can be helpful shorthand to identify what we need to do and also helpfully highlights that looking after ourselves is a habit that we can get better at. When we feel ourselves flagging, we can ask ourselves these simple questions:

P: *Do we need more practice at looking after ourselves? For example, asking for help? Or practice at politely saying no to something?*

E: *Do we need to make an effort (e.g., arranging to see a friend or to go for a walk)?*

T: *Do we need some time? It can be very hard to ask for or make time for ourselves, to attend a class or just head home, but it may be just what's needed.*

I: *Do we need further information? This could be information about work, further information about emotional wellbeing or it could be information about a hobby.*

WHEEL

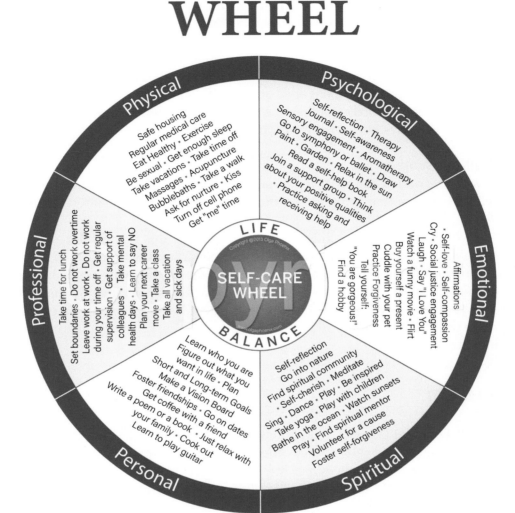

Figure 18.1 Self-care wheel

This Self-Care Wheel was inspired by and adapted from "Self-Care Assessment Worksheet" from Transforming the Pain: A Workbook on Vicarious Traumatization by Saakvitne, Pearlman & Staff of TSI/CAAP (Norton, 1996). Created by Olga Phoenix Project: Healing for Social Change (2013). Dedicated to all trauma professionals worldwide. Copyright @2013 Olga Phoenix, All Rights Reserved. Unlicensed reproduction and distribution is prohibited. Copyright licences are available for purchase at www.olgaphoenix.com

> **What do you need?**
>
> **Practise**
> **Effort**
> **Time**
> **Input**

Figure 18.2 PETI poster.

By using the PETI model we can break down the steps and make small changes to enhance our own self-care.

The everyday strategies in the table below can all be categorised using the PETI model. Not every strategy will be required by everyone, but they might be a helpful starting point.

Strategies	
TIME Offloading.	We all need to let our guard down and offload from time to time, so know who you can trust (i.e., those who will keep your confidence). This means resisting the urge to offload with those who love to spread gossip, as this may ultimately increase your anxiety. When we are tired, it can harder to resist gossiping, so know yourself and be prepared to take the consequences if you do gossip.
Effort Know your own symptoms	The more tired I become, the more I chat and the less I seem able to filter. I am, however, still responsible for everything I say, so I can't use this as an excuse. I therefore need to recognise when this is happening and do something about it. Have a think about what your symptoms are, what they're telling you and what you need to do about it.

Strategies	
Effort Leaving work at a sensible time is ok	The 'do something about it' for me is to go home at a reasonable time and have a quiet, restful night. It is ok to leave work at a sensible time. It is a job, not a life sentence.
Time Family or me time	For some, time alone or 'me time' might be needed, but, for others it could be time with friends. Whatever it is, attending to your own emotional needs is important. It also means we will be more able to support the many needs of our pupils.
Effort Ban the words 'should' and 'ought'	'Could', 'would' and sometimes 'expect' work far better, as they take away stress and give us options. 'Should' and 'ought' belong to a world where perfectionism and often unkind judgement rule leading to unnecessary anxiety and stress.
Effort Accept things might not always be perfect	Life has a rhythm all of its own. We all know that there are ups and downs, but sometimes we find it hard to accept this. Teachers in particular are very harsh towards themselves, especially if they think they've forgotten something or made a mistake. If we can accept that this is normal life, rather than 'good or bad', the consequences become easier to accept. (See 'Catch your self-criticisms' and 'Don't compare' below).
Time There is time	I had a lovely lecturer at college whose mantra was **_There is time_**. I have found that this simple phrase, said when I'm chasing my tail, has the power to calm, and is surprisingly true. Find the phrase that has a steadying effect for you and get into the habit of saying it to yourself. There will be one. I have many that I find work for different situations. (See Fig. 16.1 in Chapter 16.)
Input Use your values	Your values will have a very steadying effect. As we have explored in previous chapters if you have thoroughly thought through your values, holding yourself to account will be in light of these, rather than any external or more ephemeral judgement.

Strategies	
Effort Catch your self-criticisms	In my experience teachers are incredibly dedicated and kind to others but can be immensely hard on themselves. Begin to notice your own inner self criticism and correct it if you can. Just think of the power of adding the word 'yet' to a sentence – we do this regularly with children, so try it on yourself and hopefully you will lift a little stress.
Effort Have fun	It is ok to be cheerful and enjoy your work. Being serious all the time doesn't mean we are doing a better job. Yes, the work we do is incredibly important and can be very distressing. We must be serious at these times, but not all the time. This links with accepting the ups and downs and not getting 'stuck' in a down.
Input Don't compare and decide you are a failure.	There will always be someone better and someone not as skilled at particular aspects of our job. Comparison within education is often used as a punitive measure and, as we all know, can be incredibly destructive, if we perceive ourselves as failing. Try to appreciate and learn from those you see as 'better', and support those who may benefit from your expertise when you find you are the one who is 'better'. As long as you can genuinely say that you are working diligently, responsibly and respectfully no one can ask for more. This does not mean that you think you can't improve, in fact, quite the opposite. It values the skill of others and allows us the mental space to develop and learn from them, free from crushing, negative, 'failing' judgement. This approach positively impacts our self-worth which, in turn, lessens anxiety.
Time Use your management team	Ask for support and understanding from senior management. A brief chat over coffee might be all you need, with some empathy and understanding from a listening colleague. A compassionate, containing manager will welcome your visit. We all need appreciation, encouragement and recognition.

Strategies	
Input More resources	This could be resources for work or something more personal. A first step could be to seek further information. This links with valuing our personal needs and not allowing them to be subsumed by work.
Input Permission to get things wrong	In order for us to experience psychological safety we need to know that it's ok to make mistakes, that we can discuss them openly without the fear that we will be seen as 'not good at my job'. If we are responsible for a team, it is vital that we normalise mistakes as we would for children, rather than seeing mistakes as the end of the world.
Input Appreciation	We all need to know that we are doing a good job and that we are making a valuable contribution at work. If you are unsure, it is ok to check this out with your management team.
Input and Time Supervision	At certain times the issues that we have to deal with are exceptionally challenging and very distressing, giving rise to strong feelings, stress and anxiety. At these times you might wish to request reflective supervision. This is separate to line management and provides a safe, containing and confidential space to explore your emotions, to deal with the impact that they are having and find a constructive path ahead.

As leaders we have a duty to look after ourselves, so that we are able to carry out our role effectively but also so that our lives are more balanced and enjoyable overall. *The culture, atmosphere and environment we create will be influenced by our emotional health. We all want this to be an environment that is as free from stress and anxiety for all as possible, to create the optimum environment for learning and in order to do this we need to begin with ourselves.*

Final thoughts from the authors

We have endeavoured, through the expertise and experiences of our different careers, (1) to create a book which will resonate with primary educators and will help them understand the working of the mind of a child, whether generally anxious or suffering from more complex mental health issues, and (2) to give tried and tested practical strategies to create a containing and compassionate culture in the classroom and school and to learn about their own anxiety and stress of being a class teacher, support teacher or school leader and how to manage that. We hope that primary educators have gained more insight into the processes of human dynamics that operate in every organisation, especially schools, where adults feel the huge responsibility of educating the children in their care.

Teaching can be the most rewarding and joyful experience, and children in our schools can be helped to be freed of anxiety so that they are not only ready to learn but also able to feel the joy of confident self-efficacy. Beyond the classroom and school, an anxiety-free teacher and child can better understand, manage and seek the best in whatever life throws at them.

This book has, we hope, given all the ingredients to achieve that goal.

Shirley Clarke
Angela Evans
Kate Moss

References and recommended links

Ainsworth, M.D.S., Blehar, R.M.C., Waters, E. and Wall, S. (1978) *Patterns of Attachment: A Psychological Study of the Strange Situation*. Hillside, NJ: Erlbaum.

Barkley, R. (2020) *Taking a Charge of ADHD: The Complete Authoritative Guide for Parents*. New York: Guilford Publications.

BBC Radio 4's File on 4. (2021) *Surviving self-harm – one teenager's experience of hurting herself and a system struggling with rising demand from ever-younger children*. Download or transcript available. https://www.bbc.co.uk/sounds/play/m000s9vx

Bion, W.R. (1962) *Learning from Experience*. London: Karnac Books Ltd.

Black, P. and Wiliam, D. (1998) *Inside the Black Box: Raising Standards through Classroom Assessment*. London: King's College London School of Education.

Bowlby, J. (1944) *Forty-Four Juvenile Thieves: Their Characters and Home-life*. Reading: Bailliere, Tindall and Cox.

Bowlby, J. (1969) *Attachment and Loss: Vol. 1. Attachment*. New York: Basic Books.

Clarke, S. (2014) *Outstanding Formative Assessment*. London: Hodder Education.

Clarke, S. (2021a) *A Little Guide for Teachers: Formative Assessment*. London: Sage Publications Ltd.

Clarke, S. (2021b) *Unlocking Learning Intentions and Success Criteria*. London: Sage Publications Ltd.

Craig, M.-R. (2022) *Birdgirl*. Page 240. Colchester: Penguin Random House.

Crittenden, P. (2015) *Danger, Development and Adaptation: Seminal Papers on the Dynamic-Maturational Model of Attachment and Adaptation*. Sheffield: Waterside Press.

Diagnostic and Statistical Manual of Mental Health Disorders. (2022) *Diagnostic and Statistical Manual of Mental Health Disorders 5th edition*, text revision (DSM – 5 – TR). Washington, DC: American Psychiatric Association.

Dweck, C. (2016) How praise became a consolation prize. *The Atlantic*, December 2016.

EEF Putting Evidence to Work. (2021). https://educationendowment foundation.org.uk/education-evidence/guidance-reports/implementation

Freud, S. (1895) 'The Clinical Symptomatology of Anxiety Neurosis,' in Richards, A. and Dixon, A. (eds.) *On Psychopathology*. London: Macmillan Publishers.

Gay, P. (1995) *Freud, a Life for Our Time*. Page 281. London: Macmillan Publishers Ltd.

Geddes, H. (2006) *Attachment in the Classroom*. Duffield: Worth Publishing Ltd.

Hattie, J. (2009*) Visible Learning*. London: Routledge.

Hattie, J. (2012) *Visible Learning for Teachers*. London: Routledge.

Hattie, J. and Clarke, S. (2019) *Visible Learning Feedback*. London: Routledge.

Hickman, C. et al. (2021) Climate anxiety in children and young people and their beliefs about government responses to climate change: a global survey. *The Lancet*, 5 (12), E863–E873.

Hinz, L. (2020) *Expressive Therapies Continuum: A Framework for Using Art in Therapy*. Pages 225–227. 2nd edition. Routledge.

Kluger, A.N., and DeNisi, A. (1996) The effects of feedback interventions on performance: A historical review, a meta-analysis, and a preliminary feedback intervention theory. *Psychological Bulletin*, 119 (2), 254.

Main, M. and Solomon, J. (1986) 'Discovery of an insecure-disorganised/disoriented attachment pattern,' in Brazelton, T.B. and Yogman, M.W. (eds.) *Handbook of Attachment: Theory, Research and Clinical Applications*. Buckinghamshire: The Guilford Press.

Mandela, N. (1990/2012) *Notes to the Future: Words of Wisdom*. New York: Simon and Schuster.

Maslow, A.H. (1943) A theory of human motivation. *Psychological Review*, 50 (4), 370–396.

Maslow, A.H. (1970) *Motivation and Personality*. New York: Harper & Row.

McAnulty, D. (2020) *Diary of a Young Naturalist*. Pages 28–29. Bridport: Little Toller Books.

Mental Health of Children and Young People in England. (2017) Mental Health of Children and Young People Surveys. NHS Digital. https://files.digital.nhs.uk/A6/EA7D58/MHCYP%202017%20Summary.pdf

Meyer, W.U. (1992) Paradoxical effects of praise and criticism on perceived ability. *European Review of Social Psychology*, 3 (1), 259–283.

Morison, L., Simonds, L. and Stewart, S.-J.F. (2022) Effectiveness of creative arts-based interventions for treating children and adolescents exposed to traumatic events: a systematic review of the quantitative evidence and meta-analysis. *Arts & Health*, 14 (3), 237–262.

National College for Leadership of Schools and Children's Services. (2009) *10 Strong Claims about Successful School Leadership*. https://dera.ioe.ac.uk/2082/1/10-strong-claims-about-successful-school-leadership.pdf

Nuthall, G.A. (2007) *The Hidden Lives of Learners*. Wellington: NZCER Press.

Peters, S. (2012) *The Mind Management Programme for Confidence, Success and Happiness*. Page 159. London: Random House Group.

Report on Childhood Trust findings. (2020) https://www.bbc.co.uk/news/education-53097289

Rosenthal, R. and Jacobson, L. (1968) *Pygmalion in the Classroom: Teacher Expectation and Students' Intellectual Development*. New York: Holt, Rinehart and Winston.

Rowe, M.B. (1974) Relation of wait-time and rewards to the development of language, logic and fate control. *Journal of Research in Science Teaching*, 11 (4), 291–308.

Rubie-Davies, C. (2017) *Teacher Expectations in Education*. Oxford: Routledge.

Sellers, R., Warne, N., Pickles, A., Maughan, B., Thapar, A. and Collishaw, S. (2019) Cross-cohort change in adolescent outcomes for children with mental health problems. *The Journal of Child Psychology and Psychiatry*, 60 (7), 813–821.

Slee, A., Nazareth, I., Freemantle, N. and Horsfall, L. (2021) Trends in generalised anxiety disorders and symptoms in primary care: UK population-based cohort study. *The British Journal of Psychiatry* 218, 158–164.

Stern, D. (1977) *The First Relationship: Infant and Mother*. Cambridge: Harvard University Press.

Stigler, J.W. and Hiebert, J. (1999) *The Teaching Gap*. New York: Simon and Schuster Inc.

Willingham, D.T. (2009) *Why Don't Children Like School? A Cognitive Scientist Answers Questions about How the Mind Works and What it Means for Your Classroom*. San Francisco, CA: Jossey-Bass.

Winterson, J. (2011) *Why Be Happy When You Could Be Normal?* Pages 7, 34–35 and 76–77. London: Jonathan Cape.

Ying Sun et al. (2023) Comparison of mental health symptoms before and during the Covid-19 pandemic: evidence from a systematic review and meta-analysis of 134 cohorts. *The BMJ*, 380, e074224.

Youell, B. (2006) *The Learning Relationship – Psychoanalytic Thinking in Education*. The Tavistock Clinic Series. London: Karnac Books.

Zafirakou, A. (2023) *Lessons in Life: What We Can Learn from the World's Best Teachers*. London: Quercus Editions Ltd.

Zander, B. (2011) https://www.benjaminzander.org/library/shining-eyes-musics-power-to-connect/

https://brenebrown.com/videos/rsa-short-empathy/

https://forestschoolassociation.org/what-is-forest-school/

https://olgaphoenix.com/self-care-wheel/

https://www.mind.org.uk/information-support/tips-for-everyday-living/nature-and-mental-health/how-nature-benefits-mental-health/

https://www.thriveapproach.com

Index

Printed in the United States
by Baker & Taylor Publisher Services